AIRPLANES

OUR QUEST TO REACH THE SKIES

AIRPLANES

OUR QUEST TO REACH THE SKIES

© David E. Rowley/Envision

GARY REYES

MALLARD PRESS

MALLARD PRESS
An imprint of
BDD Promotional Book Company, Inc.
666 Fifth Avenue
New York, New York 10103

A FRIEDMAN GROUP BOOK

Published by MALLARD PRESS
An imprint of BDD Promotional Book Company, Inc.
666 Fifth Avenue
New York, New York 10103

Mallard Press and its accompanying design and logo are trademarks of
BDD Promotional Book Company, Inc.

ISBN 0-792-45261-5

AIRPLANES: *Our Quest to Reach the Skies*
was prepared and produced by
Michael Friedman Publishing Group, Inc.
15 West 26th Street
New York, New York 10010

Editor: Sharon Kalman
Art Director: Jeff Batzli
Designer: Kevin Ullrich
Photography Editor: Christopher Bain
Production: Karen L. Greenberg

Typeset by: BPE Graphics
Color separations by Kwong Ming Graphicprint Co. Ltd.
Printed and bound in Hong Kong by Leefung-Asco Printers Ltd.

The publisher wishes to acknowledge that extensive attempts have been made
to contact the holders of the copyrights on all artwork in this volume; we
apologize for any missing credits.

DEDICATION

To my grandmother, who only flew on an airplane one time in sixty-eight years, and only then so that she could see me get married.

Table of Contents

SOARING WITH THE BIRDS

Scala/Art Resource, New York

Throughout the ages, many have ignored the advice given to Icarus (left) by his father not to fly too close to the sun. Today, with gliders such as the Ultralight (opposite page), we are coming closer to soaring with the birds.

Perhaps it is impossible to know when man first felt the urge to soar with the birds. The desire to fly might have appeared first in a dream, an illusory vision of taking wing and escaping the confinements of gravity's pull. Or, to the contrary, in a moment of rational thought, the result of a calculated study of the creatures of the sky. What is known is that the attempt to duplicate the magic of the birds has filled the human spirit with equal parts of joy and sorrow throughout the course of history.

Legend has it that a King Bladud, with wings affixed to his arms, made an effort to fly sometime around 850 B.C., in what is present-day London,

Below: Many early efforts at flight began with the mistaken assumption that with a few minor adjustments, man could float on air just as the birds did.

England. It is said that the king's unfortunate attempt to fly ended tragically atop the temple of Apollo, as he plunged to his death. Whether or not the tale of King Bladud is exactly that, a tale, or an accurate description of a valiant effort to perform a feat thousands of years ahead of its time, one may never know. However, whether fact or fiction, the effort has been repeated millions of times since with success beyond our wildest dreams, and with failures equal to that of King Bladud.

Historians have recorded that around A.D. 60 Roman actors were often required to put on feathers and attempt an accurate portrayal of flight. Unfortunately, the demand for authenticity often resulted in great injury and sometimes even death. It is not known if any of the actors actually sustained flight. However, less than one hundred years later, an English monk by the name of Eilmer attached wings to his hands and feet and launched himself from the top of a tower, traveling several hundred feet, according to numerous sources. Unfortunately, Eilmer's first attempt at flight was also his last, as he broke both legs upon landing, crippling himself for life.

These early efforts at flight were limited only by the imagination and daring of the would-be birds. And not all efforts were limited to the simple donning of a pair of birdlike wings and the hurling of oneself from the top of a roof or tower. In 1420, the Venetian Giovanni da Fontana launched a rocket-powered model bird that was reported to have traveled one hundred feet (thirty meters). In 1540, João Torto of Portugal built a double-winged structure, similar in design to modern-day biplanes, and leaped from the top of the cathedral in

North Wind Picture Archive

North Wind Picture Archive

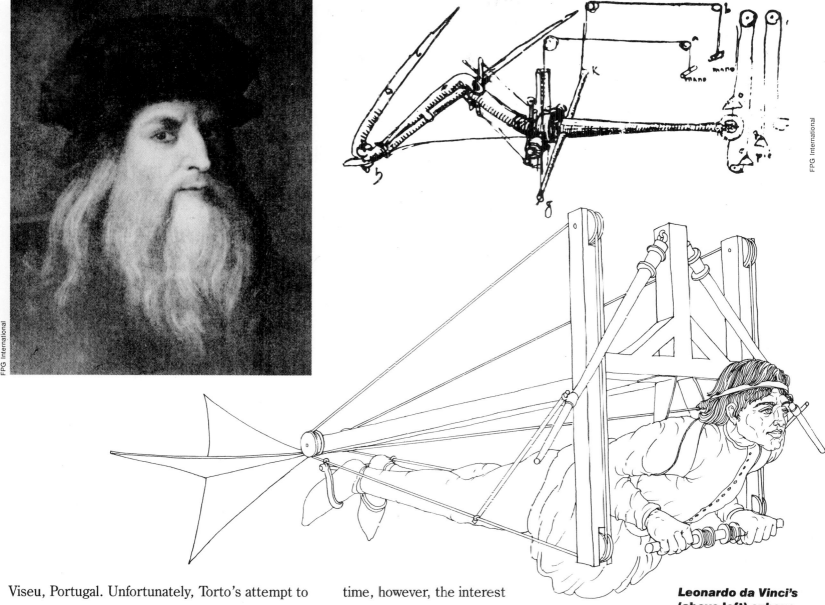

FPG International

FPG International

Leonardo da Vinci's (above left) *exhaustive study of the bird's physiology led to a greater understanding of the mechanics of flight, as well as to the design of his ornithopters (above, bottom).*

Viseu, Portugal. Unfortunately, Torto's attempt to fly ended in tragedy when the helmet he had built (to resemble the head of an eagle) slipped down over his eyes, causing him to crash fatally to the ground. Fifty years later, in Conway, Wales, John Williams took the simplest approach to flight by deploying a large overcoat in the fashion of a ship's sail. The childish nature of the idea can be explained by the fact that Williams was only seven years old at the time. Sadly, the result of young John's child's play was a duplicate of the older Torto's more calculated effort—he fell immediately to his death.

During the Middle Ages, human fascination with flight was displayed through many forms of art and literature. Angelic figures in full flight began to appear in the illustrations of religious thinkers in the late 1300s. Artists were also increasingly enamored with the idea of angels in flight. As a theatrical entertainment, court jesters simulated flying dragons with the use of ropes and pulleys. By the middle of the sixteenth century, human interest in the idea of flight had become a popular topic for writers and observers of European life. At this time, however, the interest was one of amazement more than science.

The onset of the Renaissance in Europe brought a more thorough and critical approach to the quest for an answer to the secrets of flight. Giovanni Borelli, an Italian physiologist, almost laid the quest to rest forever by stating, in his widely read treatise "On the Movement of Living Things," that "it is impossible that men should be able to fly. . . by their own strength." Despite Borelli's skepticism, his approach was significant in that it represented one of the first attempts to explain flight in rational, that is mechanical, terms. Up until the time of Borelli's study, birds in flight had been treated as a magical or mystical occurrence. By the end of the seventeenth century, his work, along with that of other rational thinkers of the Renaissance, led to a general acceptance of flight as a mechanical and physical phenomenon.

Yet another brilliant mind working in Italy during the late fifteenth and early sixteenth century was Leonardo da Vinci. Predating Borelli's work, da Vinci was also obsessed with the question of mechanics in relation to birds in flight. He found the

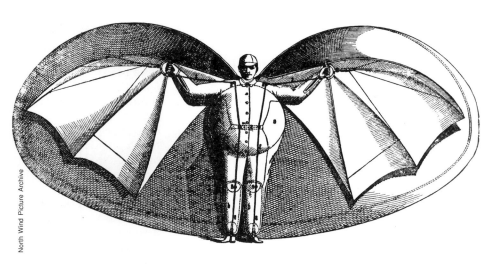

North Wind Picture Archive

that man could sustain himself in flight merely from the flapping of mechanical wings. The designs for his ornithopters (so called due to their total reliance for power on the flapping of wings) were modeled on the wings of bats. Leonardo chose this design due to his belief that a bat's wings provided the greatest amount of propulsion among all known flying creatures, due to their ability to flap down and back with differing degrees of angle. His ornithopters relied completely on hand and arm movement for power and control. It is unknown whether or not any of Leonardo's ornithopters ever attempted flight. What is known is that the desire to fly consumed his life until his death in 1519. Without the pioneering work and detailed analysis resulting from Leonardo's thirst for knowledge, the quest for manned flight might still be just that.

The fascination with flying was deeply rooted in the psyche and imaginations of scientists and inventors by the end of the seventeenth century. Historians have noted that an interest in flying kites can be traced as far back as the 1400s, when the flying of grandiose and colorful kites was a means of greeting foreign dignitaries. By the beginning of the 1600s, kites were a popular feature at English festivals and ceremonies. By no means simple in design, these kites were known to resemble various symbols of importance, such as dragons and eagles. Another event certainly related to the desire to fly was the appearance of funambulists in the mid-sixteenth century. These acrobats would attempt to entertain crowds

studies of the late fifteenth century almost useless because of their lack of an extensive examination of the physical makeup of birds. By 1505, Leonardo had completed an exhaustive and thorough study of a bird's physiology, as well as its movements in flight. He discovered that birds float on layers of air dense enough to support their weight. His further discovery—that low pressure above the wing, and high pressure below the wing provided the lift needed for a bird in flight—was a giant leap forward in the understanding of powered flight. Leonardo's pioneering work was clearly hundreds of years ahead of its time. By concentrating on a bird's ability to direct and regulate its power, Leonardo put future thinkers on the right track toward understanding the essential aspects of flight.

His study complete, Leonardo set out to transfer his empirical knowledge into practical use; he set out to fly. Unlike Borelli, Leonardo believed through simulated flight by sliding down greased ropes into cushions. With false wings attached to create a realistic effect, the popularity of these performers perhaps mirrored the dreams of the spectators to join them in flight.

With a scientific foundation for the study of flight having been laid by Leonardo and Borelli, and with increasing interest in solving the secrets of the birds from the general populace, the quest for manned flight exploded in the seventeenth and eighteenth centuries. Inventors were becoming more thorough in their practical examination of

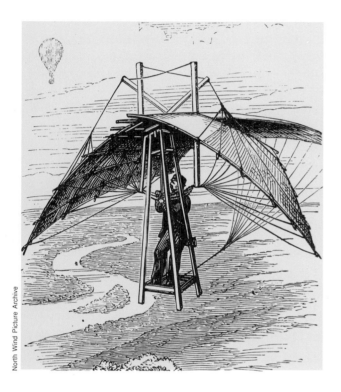

flight, and certainly more cautious in their attempts at flying itself. Adriaen Baartjens of the Netherlands donned eaglelike wings and tail (reminiscent of João Torto's fatal attempt to soar) in the mid-seventeenth century, but with one major addition; a safety line attached to prevent injury due to falling. Sometime around 1600, the Venetian Giovanni Francesco Sagredo plucked the feathers of a captured falcon in order to study its wing structure. After careful examination, Sagredo constructed a pair of wings, in direct scale to that of the falcon, for himself. A leap from a window was reported to have carried him fifty feet (fifteen meters) to a safe landing.

In 1658, following Borelli's announcement that man was incapable of self-powered flight, Robert Hooke of England suggested that manned flight may require some form of external power plant. According to Hooke, human muscles were far inferior to those of a bird for the purpose of sustaining flight. Hooke's pronouncement seems obvious by today's standards, but it was a revelation to those seeking a way to join the family of the sky, and set off a period of accelerated construction of heavier-than-air flying machines.

One of the more ambitious machines of this period came from the Italian-born scholar Tito Livio Burattini. Having already contributed to the development of the telescope, the water clock, and various measuring devices by the middle of the sev-

The most obvious way to fly: Put on a pair of wings and take off. Here are two variations on this theme, both requiring a great degree of manpower. Left: This flying parachute, a creation of Vincent de Groof, was an imitation of a bat's wings. Unfortunately for de Groof, he was thrown from it and instantly killed.

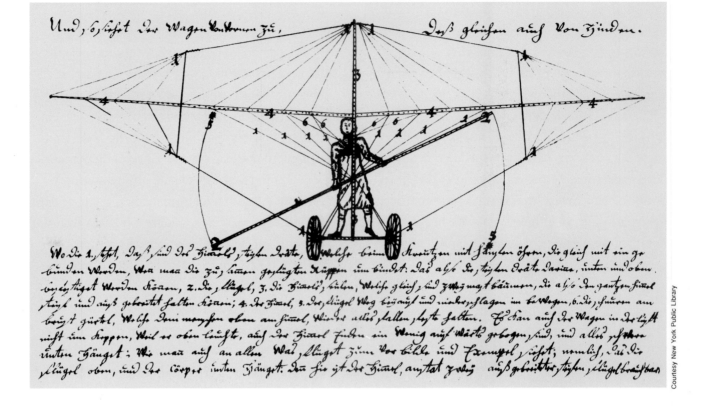

Even though Etienne Jacques Montgolfier and Joseph Michel had proven that humans were welcome in the sky (below), by the late eighteenth century, far-sighted ideas such as this design for a fixed wing aircraft by Melchior Bauer (right) received little financial support.

enteenth century, Burattini could have easily rested on his laurels. Instead, he set out to design and build a machine that would soar high and far. He chose a creature of mythical legend, the flying dragon, as the model on which he would build his air machine. Burattini's design was complex, involving the simultaneous propulsion of two master wings, four so-called lift wings, two extra wings atop the dragon's head, and a movable tail. A rod or cord was to be used to flap the wings up and down, and the entire machine was to be held together by a canopy-like cover. Three working models were constructed, including the first full-scale model of a machine specifically designed to carry humans in flight. It is not certain, however, that any of Burattini's flying dragons ever got off the ground.

Less than one hundred years later a Swede by the name of Emanuel Swedenborg set out to accomplish what Burattini had failed to do—carry a human into the sky in a man-made machine. Swedenborg's machine bore no resemblance to any flying contraption previously constructed. In fact, his machine paid greater homage to the flying saucers of modern-day science fiction than to Leonardo's ornithopter. Swedenborg draped a sailcloth over a frame made of a lightweight material such as cork, shaped in a flat, oval pattern. In this saucer-shaped machine, Swedenborg placed a cockpit in the center to house a pilot. Stretching across the middle of the saucer and attached to the cockpit were to be wide flaps that would cre-

For some, the pros-
pect of a flying ma-
chine represented an
innocent form of en-
tertainment (left and
below), while for oth-
ers, it meant a new
and more destructive
means for conduct-
ing war (above).

a permanent prison removed from earth's surface. Philosophers of the seventeenth century equated manned flight with the isolation and drudgery of a bird's life. Others were fearful of such a newfound source of superhuman power and its potential for various evil uses. Visionaries foresaw the day when wars and battles would be fought not only on land and in the sea, but in the air as well. So fearful of the consequences of flight were the citizens of France that legislation was enacted to protect the populace from the evils of men in their flying machines in the late 1700s. The laws provided that the construction of all flying machines be approved by the state, and in fact, all machines were to be state owned. One law even went as far as to require that state-approved copilots be present on all flights to ensure the lawful intention of the machine's pilot.

Of course, despite the fears and anxieties over manned flight, the quest for the sky continued. The dream that one day a human would soar with the birds would not die, although many who tried to make that dream come true did. From a fascination with the perceived magic of flight came several hundred years of small steps, finally culminating in a moment of triumph on the American shore in the early 1900s. However, without the success and failures of all who came before, we might still be waiting for that moment. To all of those who flew, to those who thought they flew, and especially to those who left life trying to fly, the world is thankful for helping bring the sky closer to the ground.

ate the lift needed to launch the craft. In the cockpit the pilot would pull on oars, identical to those in a boat, in order to cause the flaps to move up and down. As with Burattini's flying dragon, it is unknown whether or not Swedenborg's flying saucer ever got off the ground.

Overcoming the laws of physics to launch a heavier-than-air machine would prove to be an insurmountable task for the dreamers of flight prior to the nineteenth century. The accomplishments of these pioneers should not be overlooked, however, especially in light of the monumental opposition they faced from all corners of society.

Religious thinkers had long held that lifting man into the sky was a dangerous and unwanted intrusion into heaven's domain. The concept of flight was also associated with human suffering, perhaps

c h a p t e r   t w o

SCIENCE SETS ITS SIGHT ON THE SKY

With lighter-than-air balloons (opposite page and left) becoming an increasingly familiar sight in the skies over Europe during the nineteenth century, aviation gained acceptance as a scientific pursuit.

The onset of the Industrial Revolution in Europe brought a sense of legitimacy to the quest for manned flight. With society now searching for practical knowledge to further advance the cause of commerce and industry, the status of aeronautical pioneers was much improved. What had once been viewed as an inane attempt to overcome the laws of physics and gravity was now seen as a training ground for many bright and talented engineers and inventors.

One of the leaders in the march toward acceptance of aeronautical pursuit by the scientific community was the Englishman Sir George Cayley. Born during the onset of the British Industrial Revolution, Cayley developed a fascination with birds as a young boy. Like Leonardo da Vinci several centuries before, Cayley's intense study of birds in flight led him to an advanced understanding of aerodynamics. By age twenty-three, he had designed and built a flying model of a helicopter. In the early 1800s, prior to his thirtieth birthday,

Right: *Further advancing the understanding of aerodynamics, Sir George Cayley attached a pilot-operated rudder to his mid-nineteenth century glider.*

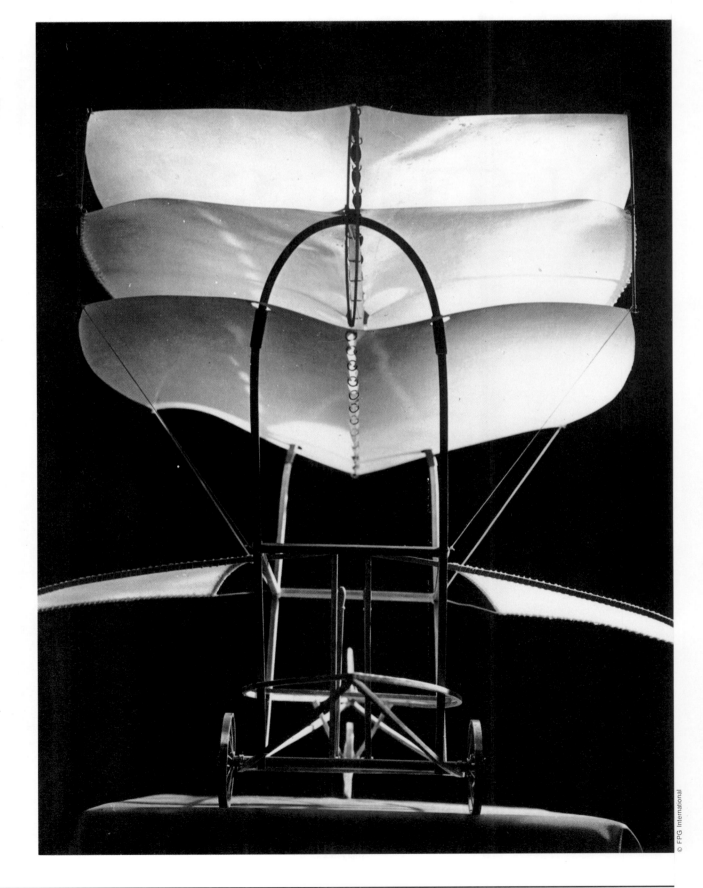

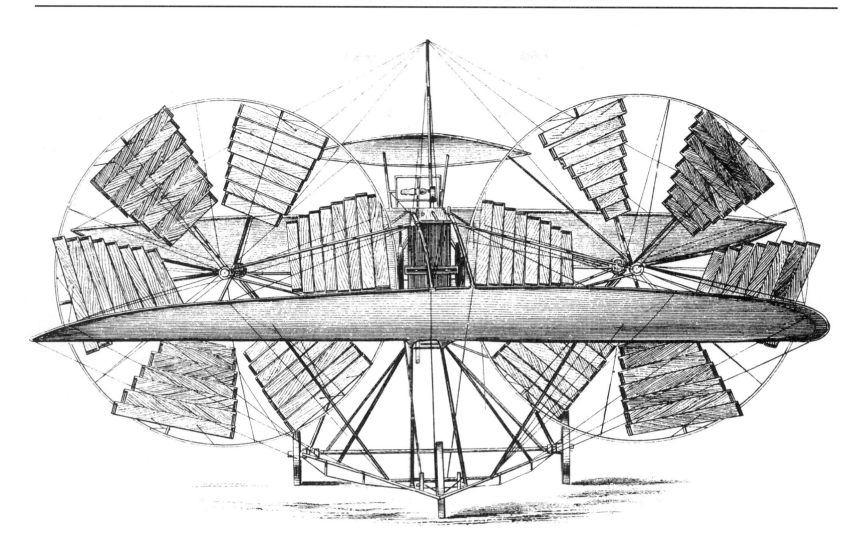

Cayley designed, built, and flew a model of a glider plane. Simple in design, the glider was little more than a paper kite connected to a tail assembly by a wooden pole. The significance of the event, however, was in the glider's ability to remain stable in the air for a prolonged period of time. Less than six years later, in 1809, the full-scale version of the glider was launched with one of Cayley's assistants on board. Whether or not the glider sustained flight is unknown. The following year Cayley published an article in a scientific journal, which explained in great detail the specifics of aerodynamics. The article aroused little interest in the scientific community, and Cayley put his efforts toward manned flight on hold for some forty years. Before he died in 1857, Cayley was able to launch his "new flyer," a glider which reportedly sustained flight long enough to cross a valley near his estate.

Perhaps Cayley's greatest contribution to the advancement of manned flight was the inspiration he provided to students of aerodynamics. One such student was a British inventor by the name of William Samuel Henson. In 1843, Henson gained a patent for what he ambitiously referred to as the "Aerial Steam Carriage." While the sky carriage was never built, it was every bit a

twentieth-century design in its detail and respect for aerodynamics. A fixed-wing monoplane with a wingspan of more than one hundred feet (thirty meters), the Aerial Steam Carriage was revolutionary in its recognition of the role of lift. Henson's design called for the wings to be angled so as to maximize their lift capability, and to be strengthened with ribs and spars. The tail assembly was to be complete with rudder and elevator, and the carriage was to be powered by twin propellers, connected to dual steam engines capable of displacing fifty horsepower. With the patent for the design secured, Henson set out to raise money for construction of the aerial carriage. His approach to raising construction funds was even

Above: *True to the teachings of Sir George Cayley, William Samuel Henson designed his Aerial Steam Carriage with an extended wingspan in order to maximize lift. Below: A detailed drawing of Henson's flying machine.*

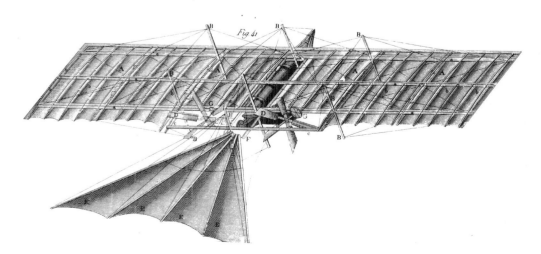

more revolutionary than his design for the carriage itself. Henson ran advertisements to lure investors into becoming shareholders in the first international airline, the Aerial Transit Company! This was the middle of the nineteenth century, fully seventy-five years ahead of the dawn of commercial aviation. Yet Henson's advertisements were very graphic in describing to the world what lay ahead in the area of intercontinental air travel. Unfortunately, few people took him seriously, and even fewer signed on as investors. Even so, Henson was able to construct and test a model of the Aerial Steam Carriage in 1847. However, the model was unable to remain airborne for more than a few seconds, and, disheartened, Henson gave up his quest to fly and moved to America.

The desire to fly was not limited to England during the nineteenth century. Several serious and calculated efforts were launched in France as well. Two Frenchmen, Count Ferdinand d'Esterno and Louis Mouillard, had concluded that unpowered manned flight was possible, given the right circumstances. Their conclusion was put to the test in 1868, when a ship captain by the name of Jean-

Marie Le Bris launched his self-built glider. Inspired by the albatross he encountered on his numerous sea voyages, Le Bris developed an intense passion to fly. His passion was so strong, in fact, that he put his career at sea on hold long enough to pursue his dream. His glider was simple in construction and design, but apparently made several successful short-duration flights during 1868.

Another man of the sea who aspired to soar with the birds was Felix Du Temple, a French naval officer. Du Temple was the designer and builder of the first powered airplane to actually fly, when the prototype for his full-scale model plane lifted off the ground and flew several feet in 1858. The propeller of his miniature airplane was powered by a most ingenious creation: a wound rubber band. Fifteen years later, Du Temple's full-scale model (powered by a steam engine, rather than a giant rubber band) made an extremely brief flight with a human at the controls.

Another pioneer of the rubber-band plane was Alphonse Penaud. Like Du Temple, Penaud was able to build a miniature plane, which he called the "planophere," capable of lifting off into the air and

While gaining in stature among the scientific community, aviation was still the dream of choice for inventors such as W. O. Ayres and his "Flying Bedframe" (right), and for the purveyors of popular culture and entertainment (opposite page).

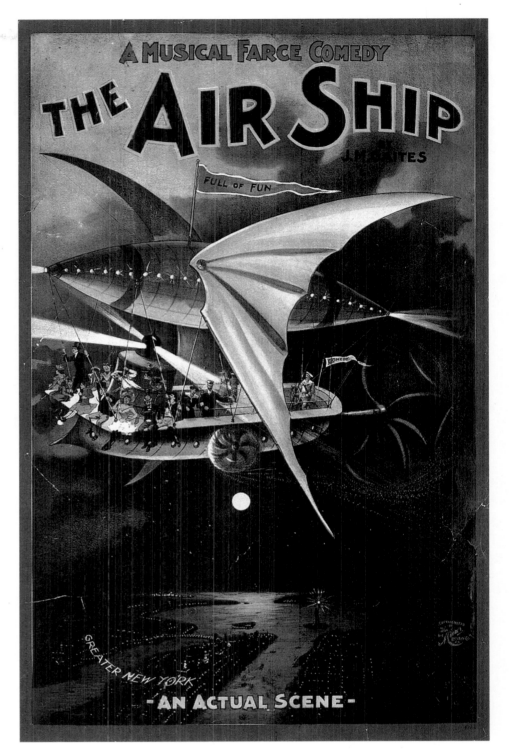

remaining airborne for a significant amount of time. Penaud's model, barely twenty inches (fifty-one centimeters) long, used a twisted rubber band to power a rear-mounted propeller. The model traveled over one hundred feet (thirty meters) in 1871, and less than five years later, Penaud was ready with a patented design for a full-scale version of an amphibious airplane. His design, however, was never realized, as he was unable to gain support from investors for his project.

A Frenchman who did find financial backing for his plan was Clement Ader. Ader reported in 1890 that he had flown his "Eole," or god of the winds, over 150 feet (thirty-seven meters). The Eole was a monoplane powered by a single twenty-horsepower steam engine. If Ader's unconfirmed report was true, he had been at the helm of the first airplane to take off from level ground under its own power. Ader's claims fell under heavy doubt a few years later, however. The French military had agreed to fund Ader's research on an airplane, resulting in the design and construction of the *Avion III,* a twin-engine airplane. The *Avion III* was bold in its design, but nonetheless failed miserably in a test flight in 1899. Needless to say, the French military withdrew their support and research money.

The most ambitious and scientific effort to put a manned aircraft into the sky came from the British

shore toward the turn of the twentieth century. Hiram Maxim was born in the United States of America in 1840. He moved to England in the 1880s due to the support from the British military for his idea on building a machine gun. Maxim's idea became a reality shortly thereafter, and the tremendous commercial success of the gun brought him quick and substantial wealth. Financially free to pursue any whim or fancy, Maxim set out to realize his childhood dream to fly. Unlike most of his predecessors, Maxim was not content to simply imitate birds in flight. His emphasis was on powering a craft capable of transporting more than just one pilot. By the early 1890s, Maxim had built a sophisticated complex for testing his flying machines, complete with a runwaylike track

While failing to realize his childhood dream to fly, Hiram Percy Maxim's (right) ambitious and calculated effort convinced many disbelievers that flight was possible. His Hiram Maxim multiplane (far right), driven by steam, was built in 1894.

FPG International

of several hundred feet. The track, which did not allow the plane to lift more than a foot or so off the ground, was put to constant use between 1892 and 1893, as Maxim repeatedly ran his airplane through one trial run after another.

The plane itself was immense in size. It was a biplane almost 200 feet (sixty meters) long, with a wingspan of over one hundred feet (thirty meters). The propellers, a whopping eighteen feet (six meters) in diameter, were powered by dual steam engines capable of generating 300 horsepower. Fully loaded with a crew of three, Maxim's biplane weighed in at an astounding four tons (3.6 metric tons). The plane made its final, but in many ways its first, true flight, in 1894. On a routine run, the track holding the plane broke down, allowing the craft to ascend briefly before it crashed to the ground, taking the dreams of Maxim's childhood with it.

The distances covered by the flying machines of the Industrial Revolution were not that much greater than those of the "tower jumpers" many centuries before. However, the leap in knowledge was as wide as an ocean. A curiosity with the wings of a bird had borne a scientific exploration of the elements of lift and propulsion. It was an exploration that would find its final realization across an ocean, the Atlantic, on the shores of an American continent teeming with its own inventors and their childhood dreams to fly.

chapter three

ONE DECEMBER MORNING ON KILL DEVIL HILLS

© John McGrail

With the dunes of Kill Devil Hills, North Carolina, providing the land (left), the Wright Brothers of Dayton, Ohio, provided the legacy of flight. Today, a monument has been erected on Kill Devil Hills (opposite page) marking the spot of the first powered flight.

Smithsonian Institution

Even though the sand dunes of the North Carolina shore were far from home for Wilbur and Orville Wright (above and below), their genius carried them to heights well beyond their humble beginnings in Dayton, Ohio (opposite page).

The dawn of the twentieth century found the relatively young United States of America poised to capture the attention of the technological world. Bright and energetic inventors were making unprecedented strides in their respective fields of endeavor. Henry Ford was on the threshold of putting millions of Americans behind the wheel of an automobile, and Thomas Edison was well on his way toward unleashing the wonders of electricity. Not to be left behind in this American parade of invention and innovation were two brothers from Dayton, Ohio, Wilbur and Orville Wright. Their pursuit, however, was perhaps the most magical of all.

It is a great wonder that the discovery of powered flight should be left to the humble sons of a Protestant minister and a mechanically adept midwestern housewife. After all, the pursuit of flight had involved the greatest minds of human history. From the earliest experiments with kites in ancient China to the amazing discoveries of Leonardo da Vinci, the quest to fly had consumed countless hours of thought among the world's most brilliant thinkers. As brilliant as they all were, however, the ultimate discovery of sustained powered flight was left to a couple of bicycle mechanics from the American Midwest.

By their early and mid-twenties, Orville and Wilbur Wright had opened a bicycle shop in their hometown of Dayton, Ohio. From the very start, this business venture was quite successful. By 1896, the Wright Cycle Company was manufacturing its own brand of bicycle, in addition to providing repair service for bicycles of other makes. Sales of Wright Cycle Company–manufactured bicycles were strong enough by the turn of the century to support a tinkering with a fancy the brothers had long held—a fancy for flight.

Like many pioneers of aviation before them, the Wright brothers had a fascination with the beauty of birds in flight. That fascination led them to collect and devour any scientific journals or other written records of attempted flight. Their collection of aeronautical information included works by the leading aviation experts of the day, such as Sir George Cayley, Alphonse Penaud, and Otto Lilienthal. The brothers were fascinated by what they

FPG International

FPG International

Above: A succession of glider flights contributed to the Wright brothers' understanding of the laws of aerodynamics.

read, but were not content to merely entertain themselves with the attempted endeavors of other aviation enthusiasts. In the first year of the new century, Wilbur and Orville Wright fixed their sights on accomplishing what others had, until that point, failed to achieve.

Like the ancient Chinese, the Wright brothers had experimented with kites. The brothers' kites, however, were more advanced to the point of revealing some secrets of aerodynamics that would allow them later to cheat the laws of physics. As a result of thorough analysis of birds in flight, the brothers constructed the wings of their kite so that they could be manipulated during turns in the air. This warping technique served to provide greater stability for the kite in flight, much akin to the role ailerons would later play in the development of the airplane. Having accomplished their initial goal of better understanding the laws of

aerodynamics, the brothers decided to put that understanding to the ultimate test.

The choice of North Carolina as a testing ground for the Wright brothers' experiments seems unusual, given that their home and business were more than 500 miles (800 kilometers) away in Ohio. The choice was a deliberate one, however, and was made with a calculating accuracy that would come to signify everything that the brothers did. After consulting various agencies and meteorological experts, the brothers chose Kill Devil Hills, near Kitty Hawk on the Outer Banks of North Carolina, because of the favorable wind and topographical features it presented. Namely, Kill Devil Hills provided the Wright brothers with an expanse of gradually declining sand dunes, free of any large hills, and visited by a constant and steady wind. An ideal setting to launch the first manned and powered airplane.

Their first trip to Kitty Hawk came in the fall of the new century, September 1900. Wilbur and Orville Wright brought their experimental glider, based on the design of their earlier kites, with the intention of staging manned test flights. The first tests were unmanned, however, due to unfavorable wind conditions. By the end of October, the winds had calmed and the brothers were sharing the honor of manning the glider on flights of more than 300 feet (ninety meters), at speeds up to twenty knots. The flights were smooth for the most part, owing to the development of an eleva-

tor on the glider's tail assembly, which provided great horizontal stability. To date, this was the Wright brothers' greatest contribution to flight. As they left Kitty Hawk for the winter, they knew it would not be their last.

Returning to Kitty Hawk eight months later, in July 1901, the Wright brothers brought with them what they hoped would be an improved glider. The new plane had an increased wing surface area, and the elevator was now in front of the plane instead of in the rear. Nonetheless, the first flights of the altered glider ended in one nose-first crash after

The winds and dunes of **Kill Devil Hills** (left) were nature's tailor-made contribution to the Wright brothers' miracle of flight.

© Chip Henderson

another. Finally, by the beginning of August, flights of just under 400 feet (122 meters) were being accomplished. Attempts to turn the glider while in flight were less successful, however, resulting in several crash landings. Knowing that maintaining flight in only one direction was of limited use, the brothers returned to Dayton very discouraged, with Wilbur predicting that "it would be another one thousand years before men and women would be able to fly."

Because they could not find a gasoline-powered engine suited to their needs, the brothers crafted their 12 horsepower engine from scratch (below).

Smithsonian Institution

Back in Dayton in the fall of 1901, the brothers turned their attention to better understanding the effects of lift on the glider's stability. To accomplish this, they constructed a wind tunnel, six feet (two meters) long and two feet (sixty centimeters) high, albeit a crude one, in which they tested a scale model of the glider's wing. The experiments in the tunnel revealed that key specifications of the glider's wing design were faulty. Nearly one year later, the brothers returned to Kitty Hawk with an even more improved glider.

Experiments in the wind tunnel indicated that a longer and more narrow wing would provide greater lift capacity for the glider. In addition, the tail assembly was redesigned to add stability by splitting the tail into two parallel parts. August of 1902 found the Wright brothers back in their compound near Kill Devil Hills with their updated glider. For the most part, the trial runs were suc-

Smithsonian Institution

Smithsonian Institution

cessful for the new plane, although problems with stall-induced spins persisted. However, with each crash landing came a better understanding of what was needed to further sustain flight. This discovery process led to the development of a rudder in the summer of 1902, which provided greater control of the glider along its vertical axis. With the rudder in place the brothers were able to make over one hundred successful flights that summer, some covering distances greater than 600 feet (180 meters). Having mastered the art of glider flight, now being able to ascend and descend, as well as negotiate turns in flight in either direction, the Wright brothers prepared to take the most logical next step—powered flight.

Upon arriving back in Dayton, a decision was made to power the next airplane with a gasoline engine. The Wright brothers believed that with the advent of the gasoline-powered automobile in America, finding an engine suitable to their needs would be easy. They were wrong. What the Wright brothers needed did not yet exist—namely, a lightweight engine capable of generating enough power to lift their glider off the ground and propel it through the air. Once again, the brothers were left to their own ingenuity in the face of a technological hurdle. And once again they responded with great success. From scratch, the brothers designed and built an engine ideally suited to their

needs. Weighing in at an amazing 140 pounds (sixty-four kilograms), the Wright brothers' engine displaced twelve horsepower from its four-cylinder configuration. They had their plane, and they now had their power source, leaving few elements of the equation yet to be solved.

Arriving at Kitty Hawk for the fourth time in September 1903, spirits were high in the Wright brothers' camp at Kill Devil Hills. The bicycle mechanics from Dayton, Ohio, had brought with them a very special and unique flying machine. Over the course of the next month, several crucial features of the plane began to develop as the brothers assembled it for the maiden voyage. Working with the tried and tested glider and the specially designed engine, the Wrights took careful steps in combining the two previously separate entities. The propellers were geared to turn in opposite directions, so as to prevent the craft from swaying. In addition, the propellers were placed in the rear of the airplane to keep any unusual air currents created from the propellers themselves behind the plane and not in front of it. By November the airplane was assembled and ready for its first flight.

On the morning of November 3, 1903 the optimism in the Wright brothers' camp was shattered. What was to be a day of great celebration and triumph turned into a day of failure and frustration. The plane suffered from mechanical difficulties

Unfortunately, the Wright brothers' first efforts at powered flight ended in failure and frustration (above).

Above: *History was made on December 17, 1903, as the Wright brothers accomplished the first manned and powered flight. Mastery of the skies belonged, temporarily, to them.*

that could not be rectified with the parts and tools on hand. With winter quickly approaching, Orville was left with few options but to return immediately to Dayton for the needed parts and tools. With the trip involving a ferry ride to the North Carolina mainland, and then several train rides, it would be several days before Orville returned to Kill Devil Hills.

Orville did return with the missing parts, and by mid-December the plane was fixed and ready for its date with destiny once again. On the morning of Thursday, December 17, 1903, the sky over Kill Devil Hills was clear. The wind (that Orville and Wilbur had intentionally sought out in coming to Kitty Hawk) was blowing at twenty knots. All in all, a pretty good day to fly an airplane. With Orville at the controls, perhaps as the result of a flip of a coin, the airplane's engine was fired up. The next ten seconds in the lives of the Wright brothers placed them forever in the annals of a select few over the course of history. Although the plane traveled less than fifty yards (forty-five meters), at an altitude barely over ten feet (three meters), aviation history had been made. The Wright broth-

Smithsonian Institution

Ford Museum

With the aviation world worshiping at their feet, the Wright brothers bid farewell to Kitty Hawk in the winter of 1903. Their flying days had only just begun, and once back in Dayton the brothers secured a farm and turned it into a training field. Here, the brothers made several successful flights in 1904 aboard *Flyer II*. By the fall of 1905, *Flyer III* was built, and would become the most prolific of the Wright brothers' airplanes. So prolific, in fact, that by the end of October, *Flyer III* was routinely making flights twenty miles (thirty-two kilometers) in duration, and staying aloft more than thirty minutes per flight.

What had begun over two thousand years before finally culminated in the human conquest of soaring with the birds. With manned flight now possible, it was up to subsequent aviators to determine the fate and future of powered flight. Having beaten his prediction by 998 years, Wilbur Wright had participated in launching the world skyward. The two bicycle mechanics from America's heartland had solved the puzzle to nature's most curious spectacle . . . flight.

ers of Dayton, Ohio, had accomplished the first manned and powered flight.

Never content to rest on their laurels, no matter how earth shattering they might be, the Wright brothers continued their experiments that very day on Kill Devil Hills. Three additional flights were made, each of longer distance than the previous one. In a fitting tribute to their shared conquest, Wilbur made the final flight of the day, and soared over 800 feet (240 meters) of the North Carolina shore, maintaining altitude for one full minute.

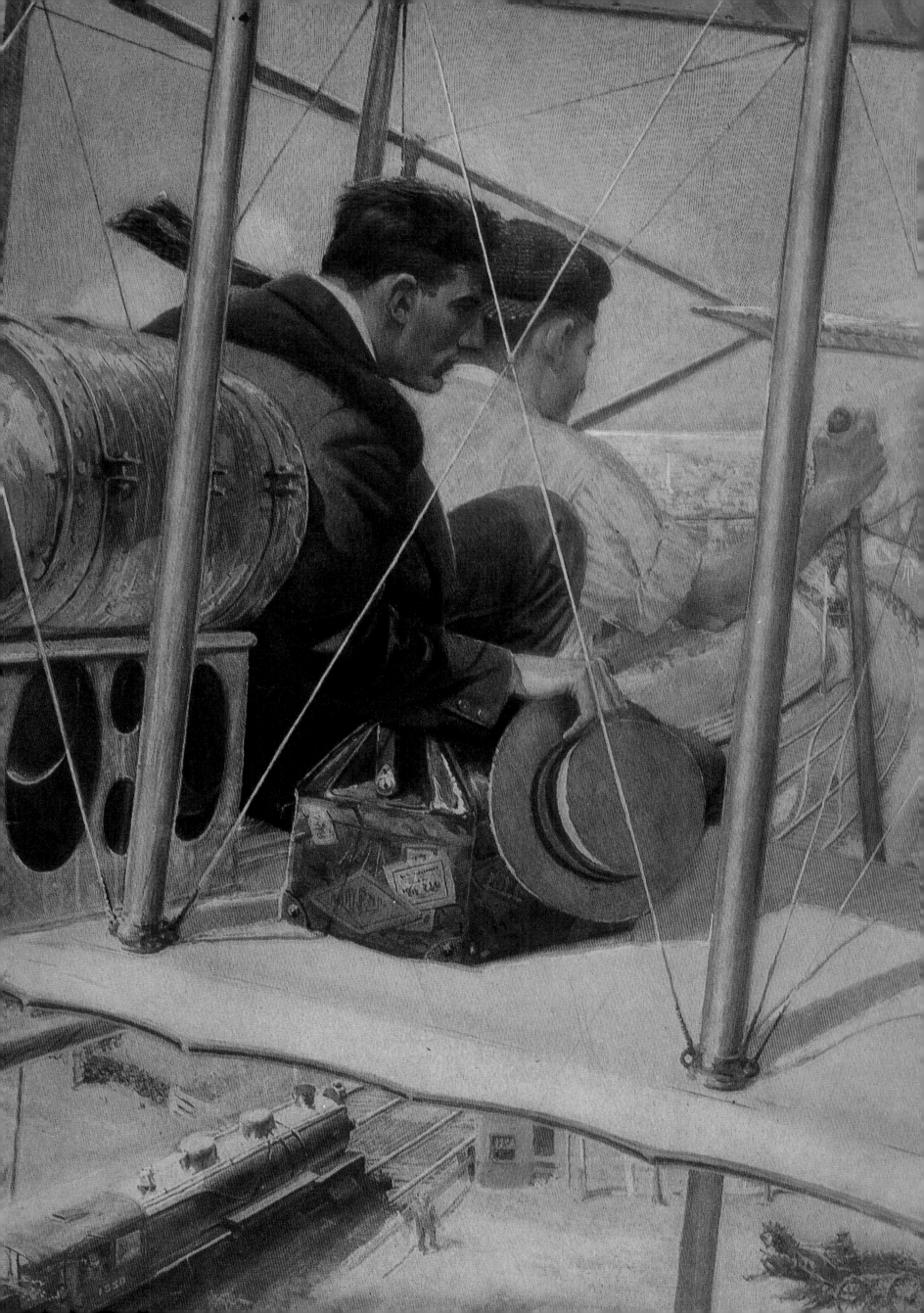

THE WORLD WANTS TO FLY

Inventions such as the Curtiss Pusher (left) advanced the dreams of aviators to someday replace the "iron horse" as the principal means of transportation in the world.

© Dick Durrance II

Smithsonian Institution

Having dazzled America with their accomplishments, the Wright brothers set out to conquer the European continent. Above is their first flight in France, during the summer of 1908.

News of the Wright brothers' accomplishments at Kitty Hawk spread rapidly. Reaction to the reports ranged from total amazement to total disbelief. From some quarters there was acceptance of the reports as fact, and consequently a rise in respect for aviation in general, and aviators in particular. But from others, including many in the scientific community, the news from Kill Devil Hills was met with skepticism. In particular, the European aeronautical community greeted the news from America with disbelief, based perhaps on a certain amount of jealousy that the discovery of the bird's secret had taken place on American, and not European, soil. Despite their reluctance to accept the Wright brothers' claims as fact, the news from across the ocean launched the European continent on an accelerated, almost frantic pace to build and fly a powered airplane.

For the most part, Wilbur and Orville Wright cared very little about what the rest of the world thought of their airborne exploits. The attainment

Ford Museum

of publicity and fame were not the driving goals behind the brothers' pursuit of manned flight. They were, however, very concerned with protecting their discovery from unauthorized commercial exploitation. Toward that end, Wilbur made a trip to Europe in the summer of 1908. His goal was to set up joint production of Wright airplanes with a group of French investors. The investors were extremely interested in the prospect of building flying machines, but were also somewhat skeptical of the Wright brothers' claims of success in the air. As a group, they demanded to see a demonstration flight from Wilbur. In August of that year he obliged.

In a field near Le Mans, France, Wilbur Wright made a two-minute flight that astonished the crowd. Like any great performance, his brief outing in the air left the crowd wanting more. Over the next month, Wilbur obliged his hosts by flying on an almost daily basis, culminating with a flight on September 21, 1908, which set a new endurance record of just over one hour and thirty minutes. Needless to say, Wilbur had succeeded in convincing his investors, as well as the entire European continent, that the accomplishments of he and his brother were real. The demonstration flights served another crucial purpose that summer in France, as members of the viewing public grew to include many future aviators who had been unsuccessful in their own efforts at flight up until that point. The unusual openness of the demonstration flights proved to solve many design secrets for these aviators, as they got a firsthand glimpse of the Wright brothers' airplane and all of its aeronautical marvels.

One of the first French aviation pioneers to borrow from the Wright brothers' design was a wealthy automotive engineer by the name of Louis Blériot. Blériot was by no means a newcomer to the quest for flight. By the time Wilbur made his demonstration flights in France in 1908, Blériot had managed to build more than ten flyable airplanes. Unfortunately, he was also able to destroy just as many due to his acute lack of attention to the intricacies and details of aerodynamics. Blériot was extremely enthusiastic and anxious to fly—perhaps too anxious. His lack of patience, and failure to heed advice from his mechanical staff, left him bankrupt by the end of 1908 from one failed aerial exploit after another.

Not to be outdone by the upstart Americans, Frenchman Louis Blériot (below) led the European assault on the aviation record books, becoming the first man to fly across the English Channel.

Blériot's crossing of the English Channel made him an instant international celebrity. Here (right), his plane is seen flying over the cliffs of Dover.

©Terry Gwynn-Jones Collection

©Terry Gwynn-Jones Collection

Above: Before Blériot accomplished his crossing of the English Channel in 1909, Gustav Hamel Gives attempted the same flight in 1902. Left: American Harriet Quimby became the first woman to cross the English Channel in 1911. The streamlined design of the French-built Deperdussin allowed it to dominate aerial speed records in 1912.

History and a great deal of luck were on the side of Louis Blériot, however. The Wright demonstration provided his engineering team with crucial information on maintaining lateral stability in the air. At almost the same time, his wife inherited a considerable amount of money, allowing him to continue his pursuit of the sky. His dogged pursuit paid off handsomely in the summer of 1909. Chasing a five-thousand-dollar prize that had been put up by a British newspaper, Blériot set out to accomplish what must have seemed impossible to most—crossing the English Channel by air. On July 25, 1909, after several unsuccessful attempts, Blériot realized his dream. He became the first aviator to leave French soil and land on the English shore. Although his voyage from

Sangatte to Dover barely covered thirty miles (forty-eight kilometers), his forty minutes airborne over the churning waters of the English Channel served to further feed the frenzy for aviation developing throughout Europe.

Blériot's feat helped propel Europe into a state of air supremacy over America, a supremacy they would enjoy for the next decade. Beginning in 1911, each new aviation record seemed to belong to Europe, and in particular to the great aviators of France. The year 1911 saw Roland Garros set a new world altitude record of 12,800 feet (3,900 meters). More importantly, his record was accomplished in a French-designed and -built airplane, not in a Wright-built model. The records for speed and endurance also belonged to France that year.

ROUTE OF C.P. RODGERS IN HIS VIN FIZ — WORLD'S RECORD FLIGHT FROM COAST to COAST

5¢ THE IDEAL DRINK

Flying a Wright-built airplane, Calbraith Perry Rodgers spanned the American continent. This poster (above) celebrates the crossing.

Speeds eclipsing eighty miles (130 kilometers) per hour had been attained in airplanes designed by the Frenchman Edouard Nieuport, while distances covered on a single flight exceeded 460 miles (740 kilometers). Clearly the Europeans had made up for lost time in the global race for air superiority.

While the Wright brothers' main competition for control of the skies was in Europe, there were competitive forces emerging at home as well. In his failed attempt to beat the Wright brothers to the sky, the brilliant Smithsonian scientist, Samuel Langley, had attempted to launch his *Aerodrome* from a catapult in December 1903. The plane plunged into the Potomac River almost immediately, thereby bringing to an end the seventy-year-old Langley's race with the Wrights. Progress was slow for most American aviators throughout the rest of the decade, although there were isolated streaks of brilliance.

Calbraith Perry Rodgers provided one of the greatest feats of American aviation history in

1911. From Sheepshead Bay, New York, Rodgers set out in September 1911 to cross the American continent. Navigating his Wright-built airplane by following railroad tracks, he reached Long Beach, California, twelve weeks later, having covered some 4,000 miles (6,400 kilometers). Rodgers's moment in glory was brief but significant, given the fact that only two years earlier great acclaim and honors had been heaped on Blériot for crossing a mere thirty-mile (forty-eight kilometer) channel.

The American that would prove to be the most formidable challenge to the Wright brothers was himself a bicycle mechanic. Glenn Curtiss, born and raised in upstate New York, shared not only the same vocation as the Wrights, but their thirst to fly as well. By the time he reached his thirtieth birthday, Curtiss had demonstrated his penchant for adventure. In 1907 the bicycle mechanic from New York set a world land speed record of 136 miles (218 kilometers) per hour at Ormond Beach, Florida . . . on a motorcycle. The relative

Calbraith Perry Rodgers brought the miracle of aviation to almost every corner of the Continental United States (above and left).

safety of the earth's surface was not enough to quench Curtiss's desire for adventure, and by the end of 1907 he served notice of his intentions to conquer the sky as well.

Teaming with one of the great minds of all time, Alexander Graham Bell, Curtiss established a company in 1907 with the intention of developing an airplane. Throughout 1908, Curtiss made several successful flights in various airplanes designed and built by the new company. His association with Bell ended abruptly, however, and in 1909 Curtiss took on a new partner. The resulting company became the first established commercial airplane manufacturer in the United States. By June of that year, the Herring-Curtiss *Golden Flyer* was made available to the public for the first time. For five thousand dollars, trained pilots and amateur daredevils alike could now be lucky enough to own their own airplane. As the first offering out of the factory, the *Golden Flyer* was quite a piece of machinery. With a wingspan of twenty-nine feet (nine meters), and a thirty-horsepower engine, the plane weighed in at a relatively light 550 pounds (250 kilograms).

In August 1909, Curtiss thrust himself into the international limelight of the rising class of glamorous stars known as aviators. By winning the endurance race at the Rheims Air Show, far and away the most significant public event staged in aviation history up until that point, Curtiss gained worldwide recognition for himself and his company. His success at Rheims, however, as well as that of his

His daring surpassed only by his ambition, Glenn Curtiss (inset left) led the challenge against the Wright brothers for superiority in the American skies. Overleaf: The object of the Wright brothers' wrath: Glenn Curtiss and his biplane. The feud between the brothers and Curtiss led to a lawsuit that dragged on for years, eventually contributing to the early death of Wilbur Wright.

The Curtiss influence on American aviation was far-reaching. Whether piloting the Langley Aerodrome (below) or providing engines for the early works of the brilliant Lougheed brothers, Glenn Curtiss asserted himself quickly and forcefully in American aviation circles.

predominantly European counterparts, was overshadowed somewhat by events on the ground back home in the United States. Taking the offensive in their battle against what they perceived as blatant patent infringement, the Wright brothers began a series of legal maneuvers that would unfortunately drag on for many years. In many ways, America's advancement in the skies would be dragged down as well.

The actual Wright brothers case against Glenn Curtiss began in 1910. While both sides would realize victories during various stages of the case, the overall result was a sapping of valuable creative energies from both sets of participants. Neither Curtiss nor the Wright brothers would realize great success in the air after the legal battle began on the ground in 1910. The biggest blow from the feud was felt in 1912, when Wilbur Wright died at

the young age of forty-five. Although the cause of death was medically attributed to typhoid, the Wright family clearly pointed to another source as the cause of Wilbur's ill health—Glenn Curtiss.

The ultimate resolution to the patent war between the two giants of American aviation took place outside the courtroom altogether. The legal fight raged on up until the eve of American entry into World War I. At that point, a greater concern intervened to bring the Wright-Curtiss dispute to a close, the concern for America's survival. By war-induced government order, patents for all war-related technologies were collectivized. Less than fifteen years after the Wright brothers' success at Kitty Hawk, the world would get to see the wonders of aviation used for purposes only earlier visionaries had imagined, but the dreamers never intended—for war.

Above: *The Lougheed Model G, featuring an 80 horsepower Curtiss engine and consisting of fabric stretched and glued over a wooden frame, was the first effort of Allan and Malcolm Lougheed.*

chapter   five

THE AIRPLANE GOES TO WAR

Two inventions in relative infancy, the airplane (left) and the machine gun (opposite page) combined to add new meaning to the wishes of aviators to conquer the sky during World War I.

The great thinkers of the Renaissance had worried about the potential evils of manned flight. Legislators in France had gone so far as to enact laws protecting society from the unknown depths to which man would fall once he gained command of the sky. For the most part, the legislation was folly. The concerns that prompted the legislation were not. As the world would witness during the nightmare of the First World War, taking battles into the sky brought even more widespread destruction than the thinkers of several centuries before had envisioned.

In 1913, a young Frenchman by the name of Adolphe Pegoud was thrilling crowds across Europe with his daring feats of airborne acrobatics. Aviation history counts Pegoud as the pioneer of such aerial maneuvers as the loop, the rollover, and the controlled midair stall. Pegoud's feats are made even more remarkable by the fact that they were accomplished in aircraft designed to meet the basic requirements of flight, not the gravity-defying feats of aerial maneuvers. Structural miracles notwithstanding, Pegoud's courage and risk-

Intended merely as crowd pleasers, the aerial feats of Adolphe Pegoud (below) would soon be put to use in the air battles fought over Europe in World War I. Right: Pegoud is seen flying upside down, a feat he was the first to try.

taking broke new ground in the continual discovery of the airplane's many uses. Unknown at the time was that Pegoud's thrill-seeking stunts would become standard operating procedure for military pilots around the world; pilots found themselves using Pegoud's maneuvers to elude, chase, and kill each other a few years later. It is both ironic and tragic that Pegoud died at the hands of a German fighter plane near Alsace, at age twenty-six.

While Pegoud gets credit for inventing, knowingly or not, the maneuvers that became commonplace among military pilots across Europe, he does not get total credit for inventing the military use of aircraft in general. That credit is shared by several aviation pioneers who recognized the tremendous potential an airplane represented in the military arena.

As early as 1910, American aviators had begun to experiment with the possible military uses for the airplane. In November of that year, American pilot Eugene Ely conducted the first successful takeoff of an airplane from the deck of a ship, the U.S.S. *Birmingham,* near Hampton Roads, Virginia. Two months later, Ely landed his Curtiss biplane on the deck of the U.S.S. *Pennsylvania,* anchored in San Francisco Bay. In addition to Ely's feats of early 1911, American pilots had also experimented for the first time with the dropping of live explosives from aircraft in flight. A year later in St. Louis, Missouri, Captain Albert Berry

Above: *Eugene Ely demonstrates the airplane's naval utility, as he completes the first successful takeoff from the deck of a ship.*

jumped from a Benoist aircraft at 1500 feet (457 meters), and became the first man to land safely using a parachute. Finally, in 1912, a machine gun was mounted onto a Wright biplane for the first time, leaving little to the imagination as to its intended use. Clearly the airplane was being outfitted for non-civilian uses.

In fact, as early as 1909 the Wright brothers had been actively courting the military market in the United States and Europe. The Wright Mili-

tary Flyer was a two-seater biplane in which the second man on board served either as a scout or as a gunner. The Wright brothers' efforts paid off in 1909, when the Military Flyer became the first airplane acquired by the United States Army. Two years later, the Wright brothers' main competitor, Glenn Curtiss, debuted his Curtiss A-1. With its underwing floats, the A-1 had the distinction of becoming the first seaplane and the first aircraft in the United States Navy. The Curtiss A-1 captured

With the introduction of the Wright Military Flyer (below), militarization of the airplane soon found it in the skies as well as at sea. However, in order for the Flyer to land on a naval vessel, it was necessary to construct a special platform (right).

FPG International

FPG International

another distinction two years later when the plane engaged in the first military confrontation involving an American aircraft. Five A-1s from the U.S.S. *Mississippi* and the U.S.S. *Birmingham* came under small-arms fire while flying reconnaissance missions over Vera Cruz, Mexico, in April 1914. Up until that point, isolation from the troubles brewing on the European continent had led to a lack of enthusiasm for developing military aircraft in the United States. The events of 1914 and 1915 shattered that sense of false security, however, as America joined the race to secure superiority in the skies.

It was clear as early as 1910 that Europeans had seized the lead in aviation technology from the Americans. This superiority was nowhere more evident than in the application of military uses for the airplane. In its war against Turkey for control of North Africa, Italy had used airplanes for scouting and bombing missions in 1911. By 1912, the

Royal Flying Corps had been founded in England, while in France, an air force of over 250 planes was already in existence. While the Germans trailed France and England in the development of military airplanes, Count Ferdinand von Zeppelin ensured a military presence in the sky for Germany with the development of his dirigibles. Even the Far East got a taste of the increasingly militarized skies, as China took delivery of twelve French Caudrons in 1913.

While America had the Wright brothers and Glenn Curtiss, Europe, too, had its share of daring personalities driving the discovery of aviation's wonders. While the Wrights challenged Glenn Curtiss in court, the designers and builders of European airplanes would have a more telling and more deadly arena in which to test one another: the skies over Europe. The inventors, engineers, and daredevil pilots of World War I Europe left an eternal mark on the history of aviation. The men

Extending his influence beyond civil aviation, Glenn Curtiss delivered his Flying Boats (below) to the United States Navy in 1911.

With help from the adventurous Samuel Cody (below), an English army aviator, the British aviation effort quickly evolved from sluggish dirigibles (right).

and machines of 1915 to 1919 are as recognizable today as they were during the battles for control of the skies over Europe during World War I.

In England, a native American by the name of Samuel Cody launched the British skyward in 1908. The former horse trader from Texas became the first to fly a heavier-than-air machine with the successful flight of his British Army Aeroplane Number 1. More importantly, Cody assisted the British army in the design and construction of military dirigibles before his death.

A trio of brothers native to England contributed greatly to the war cause with the development of several naval aircraft. Eustace, Hugh, and Horace Short designed the folding wing aircraft that allowed the British navy to utilize the maximum number of aircraft in battle.

Having helped design the double-decker buses that traveled on London streets, Geoffrey de Havilland turned his attention toward building aircraft in the early twentieth century. The results of his efforts were crucial to the aerial successes enjoyed by the British in World War I. After its debut in 1913, de Havilland's Blériot Scout Number 1 quickly became the prototype for future fighter planes. With its 100-horsepower engine, the biplane was capable of exceeding ninety miles (144

kilometers) per hour, due in large part to the reduction in drag created by encasing the cowling, rather than leaving it exposed.

Perhaps the key figure in British aviation during World War I was an engineer by the name of Thomas Sopwith. Sopwith's Tabloid appeared in 1913, and immediately garnered attention because of its performance capabilities. Sopwith's biplane was capable of ascending at a remarkable 1,500 feet (457 meters) per minute. In later design stages the Tabloid became the Camel, capable of speeds up to 110 miles (176 kilometers) per hour, and an extremely crucial element in the British war arsenal.

Below: *The speedy and versatile Sopwith Pup, built by Thomas Sopwith. Overleaf: World War I brought the fears of many earlier thinkers to reality, as the airplane became the newest member of an Army's arsenal.*

© James N. Reuss

© Frank B. Mormillo
© Frank B. Mormillo

Proving themselves equal to the challenge of the British Sopwiths (below, right and far right), the German air forces were bolstered by the designs of Anthony Fokker (above) and the piloting skills of Manfred von Richtofen (far left and left).

© Frank B. Mormillo

Above: Anthony Fokker, an important and influential force in German aviation. Not to be outdone in the air, Russian airplanes such as the Sikorsky Muromet (below and opposite page, above), and the Moraine monoplanes of the French Air Force (opposite page, below), proved that no nation had a monopoly on designing and building military aircraft. Overleaf: Still a beautiful machine, airplanes such as this Fokker monoplane became war planes with the simple addition of a mounted machine gun.

While England and France led Europe in airplane production during the early stages of the war, several other countries achieved success in the air before the war ended. Anthony Fokker, a Dutch aristocrat studying engineering in Germany, built and flew a crude monoplane in 1910. His brilliance and determination to fly resulted in the construction of the M.5 in 1913. Humble in its first appearance, the M.5 evolved into a superior fighter plane and achieved great success in air battles over France during the war.

Aircraft development was certainly not limited to small fighter planes during World War I, as witnessed by the Taube and the Russky Vityaz. Designed by Austrian Igo Etrich, the Taube bomber became the first airplane to release explosives in a wartime setting, when Italy used it for such purposes in North Africa. The Taube later had the distinction of making the first bombing run on a major city, when Germany launched an aerial assault on Paris in August 1914. The Russky Vityaz, designed by Russian-born American Igor Sikorsky, held two distinctions upon its debut in 1913. It was the first so-called heavy bomber, and the first military aircraft to utilize four engines.

All in all, the nations of Europe were relatively well equipped to do battle in the sky when war officially broke out in August 1914. With Germany declaring war against Russia and France in January, followed four months later by the declaration of the Austro-Hungarian Empire against England, the European continent was once again engaged in a struggle for military superiority. Only this time,

the struggle would be fought on land, at sea, and in the air.

At the outset of the war, England and France had well over 1,500 aircraft at their disposal. Germany trailed with just over 1,000. The first casualties of the air war were quick in coming. By August 1914, both England and Germany had suffered losses in the sky, with the British losing an Avro 504 to small-arms fire in Belgium, and the Germans losing an Aviatik near Rheims, France. The first Austrian loss also came in August when a Morane-Saulnier monoplane of the Russian air force rammed and destroyed an Austrian fighter plane. Before 1914 ended, British Sopwith Tabloids were making bombing runs on German cities well behind the front lines of the war. Never before in the history of warfare had behind-the-line positions been so endangered and so difficult to defend.

As the war dragged on, the names and feats of the aces of the sky and the machines they commanded quickly achieved legendary status. Roland Garros of France became an even greater legend in April 1915, after gunning down an Albatros and four other German aircraft with his Hotchkiss machine gun mounted to the Morane-Saulnier monoplane he was piloting. Victory at sea became an even greater feat when a Short 84 seaplane was able to sink a Turkish ship using an aerial-dropped torpedo. The British enjoyed additional success on the open waters when sea-launched Sopwith Pups were able to engage in airborne dogfights closer to enemy lines.

Smithsonian Institution

Patrick Walmsley/Envision

Obtaining greater speed and maneuverability was the goal of military aircraft designers during World War I. Two of the more successful efforts were the Scouting Experimental-5 (opposite page, above) of the Royal Aircraft Company, and the French-built Nieuport 17 (below). While the SE-5 gained speed from the power of its Hispano-Suizo engine, the Nieuport 17 employed a smaller, almost nonexistent lower wind to give it an advantage during aerial maneuvers. Equal in importance to the airplane's design, of course, was the skill of the pilot. Few possessed greater natural talent for flying than the American Ace Eddie Rickenbacker (above).

While the aviation feats of the early war years had an adventurous and somewhat harmless feel to them, the destruction that rained from the skies toward the end of the war shattered the romantic myth of the airplane. In May 1917, twenty German Gotha G IV bombers launched a daylight assault on the British city of Kent. Ninety people were killed, and well over 200 were injured. Less than one month later, another Gotha raid left 150 dead in London. No longer was the airplane a magical mixture of technology to be marveled. Instead, in just a few short years it had become a feared and dreaded weapon, capable of delivering death and destruction to the shores of any nation on earth.

While men and machines died in the war, others survived to carry the legacy of aviation into the postwar years. Rittmeister Manfred Freiherr von Richtofen—otherwise known as the "Red Baron"—did not live beyond his glorious moments in the aerial battles of World War I. Nor did the great Frenchman Adolphe Pegoud. But the names of those who did survive—Rickenbacker, Fokker, and de Havilland—continued the advancement of aviation around the world. By war's end, the Royal Air Force alone found itself with over 500 airfields, 22,000 airplanes, and countless numbers of trained pilots reluctant to retire from flying at such an early age. The new challenge to the world was to find a peaceful and beneficial use for the now-proven mechanical birds of the sky.

AIR MAIL
is Socially Correct

5¢ for the **First Ounce**   10¢ for each additional **Ounce**

c h a p t e r   s i x

FROM BOMBING RUNS TO MAIL RUNS

Sending mail through the air added a sense of glamor and civility to an otherwise mundane task.

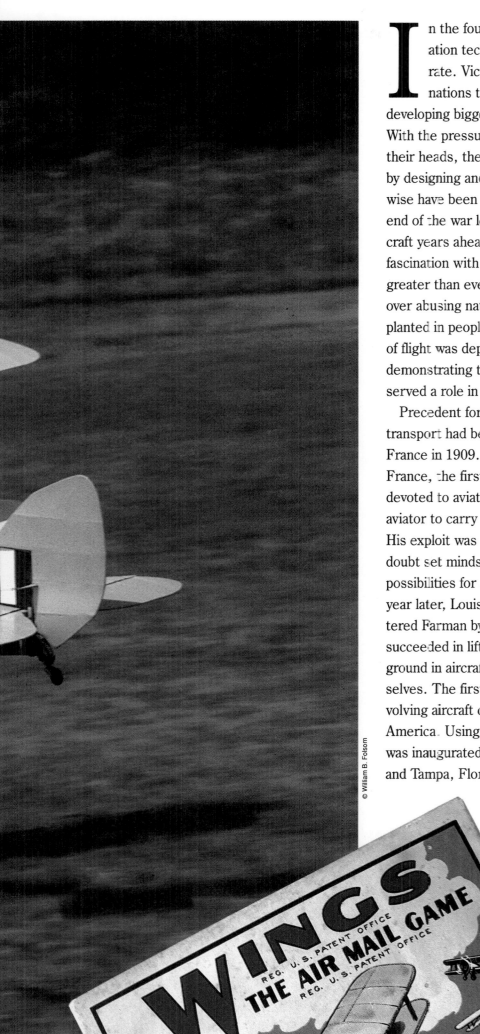

© William B. Folsom

In the four years spanning World War I, aviation technology grew at an unprecedented rate. Victory in the sky required warring nations to devote their resources toward developing bigger, faster, and stronger airplanes. With the pressure of military defeat looming over their heads, the nations at war met this challenge by designing and building aircraft that might otherwise have been generations away. As a result, the end of the war left the world with a surplus of aircraft years ahead of current needs and uses. The fascination with machines that flew in the sky was greater than ever, although fears and anxieties over abusing nature's secret had now been forever planted in people's minds. Once again, the future of flight was dependent upon aviation pioneers demonstrating to the world that the airplane deserved a role in their everyday lives.

Precedent for using the airplane as a human transport had been set by Henry Farman of France in 1909. At the air show at Rheims, France, the first international gathering strictly devoted to aviation, Farman had become the first aviator to carry more than one passenger aloft. His exploit was strictly noncommercial, but no doubt set minds in motion over the money-making possibilities for aerial transport. Less than one year later, Louis Breguet and Roger Sommer bettered Farman by nine passengers, as they both succeeded in lifting eleven passengers off the ground in aircraft they designed and built themselves. The first scheduled passenger service involving aircraft came less than two years later in America. Using Benoist Flying Boats, air service was inaugurated between St. Petersburg, Florida, and Tampa, Florida, in February 1914. The pas-

Peacetime uses for aircraft, such as the de Havilland Tiger Moth (left), inspired games on the ground (below).

71

senger and freight service only covered twenty-two miles (thirty-five kilometers) and was short-lived, but the example had been set. While the role of the airplane as a means of transportation was developing, other uses were beginning to come into focus even before World War I began. As early as 1910, using Blériot monoplanes, the British established a system of carrying the mail through the air. Wartime hostilities brought all peaceful developments to a halt as the airplane was drafted into the ranks of military service.

In the immediate postwar period, several factors were working against the widespread expansion of aviation, particularly in the United States. Unlike the European continent, North America had precious few airfields in existence or under construction. There were even fewer full-service airports ready to handle passengers and freight. Even if the airports had been in existence, the methods by which planes would find and land at these facilities were primitive at best. Navigational systems were still many years away, and navigating according to the roads was not exact, as the American road system was also in its infancy. Had there been airfields to land on and navigational systems to find them, there was still the problem

Below: The cockpit of the Vickers Vimy, the plane in which John Alcock and Arthur Brown made a transatlantic flight.

Left: *With a less-than-picture-perfect landing in Ireland, Alcock and Brown spanned the Atlantic non-stop, departing from Newfoundland and landing in Ireland nearly sixteen hours later.*

of passenger aircraft, or lack thereof. In the first twenty years of the century, aviation technology had grown by leaps and bounds, but had not yet provided a reliable civilian transport. Compounding these problems was the precarious financial situation that the combatant nations of the First World War found themselves in once the conflict had ended. Funds for rebuilding war-ravaged economies did not extend to the developing of an aviation industry.

Nonetheless, aviation-related businesses managed to develop and grow. Spurred on by government action and individual feats of aerial daring, the aviation industry rose from the ashes of World War I. In June 1919, the British flying team of John Alcock and Arthur Brown stunned the world. Aboard a converted bomber, a Vickers Vimy, the duo took off from Newfoundland and landed in Ireland less than sixteen hours later. The first non-stop transatlantic flight showed the world how the airplane could bring people and places closer to one another faster than ever before. Shortly thereafter, the first scheduled airline service was established between England and the European continent. Regular service aboard de Havilland DH-4s and DH-6s began in August 1919, linking London and Paris. Founded by George Holt Thomas, the Aircraft Transport and Travel Company offered passage for two and four passengers at a time on the two-hour trip across the Channel. One month later, the Handley Page Transport Company began competing service between London and Paris. Seating for two (in an enclosed

Smithsonian Institution

Decades away from the advent of overnight mail, surplus aircraft from World War I, and the pilots that flew them, brought the world even closer in its march to becoming a "global village."

cabin), was offered aboard Handley Page 0/400s that had been used as bombers during World War I. Before the year was out, another scheduled carrier, Intone Air Line, extended air service from London to Brussels, Belgium, and Cologne, Germany, using converted Vickers Vimy bombers.

England was certainly not the only home to pioneering air carriers in Europe. KLM Royal Dutch began regular service in October 1919, followed closely by Danish Airlines in August 1920 (which evolved into SAS Scandinavian Airline), and the

Belgian carrier SNETA (later to be known as Sabena-Belgian World Airlines) in 1923. By 1926, two German carriers, Deutscher Aero Lloyd and Junkers Luftverkehr, had merged into eventual airline giant Deutsche Lufthansa. As far away as Australia, the Queensland and Northern Territory Aerial Services (QANTAS) was founded in November 1920. It was in England, however, that the first major international carrier was formed. In 1922, Daimler Airway began service between London and Berlin using de Havilland DH-34 aircraft. In March 1924, the British government merged Daimler with Handley Page Transport, Intone, and Marine Air to form Imperial Airways. In a matter of years, Imperial Airways performed the impossible feat of reaching to every corner of the globe.

While air transportation was growing rapidly in Europe, development was slower in the United States. By flying coast to coast in a DH-4 in just

over twenty-two hours in 1922, James Doolittle made an important point. For any individual or business sensitive to the demands of time, Doolittle's feat had special meaning. With American businesses spreading out across the country to reach new customers, any and all means to speed up contact between producer and consumer was welcome. Improved telecommunication links now allowed main offices to be connected with factories and satellite offices in the field. Face-to-face communication was still a matter of necessity, and travel times could be cut in half traveling by air. As a means of transporting time-sensitive products and business personnel, air travel offered the best of all worlds. The problem faced, however, was building airplanes to fulfill the potential.

Because of the low demand for aircraft in the immediate postwar years, early American aviation industrialists were forced to rely on remnants from the war itself. By 1920, the United States Postal Service had implemented coast-to-coast service via airmail. Surplus de Havilland DH-4s could carry mail from New York to San Francisco in just over three days; by land, this could take ten days. Other military aircraft adopted for civilian duty included the French Farman Goliath and the Vickers Vimy. The Goliath first appeared as a bomber in 1918. After slight modifications, the all-wood twin-engine biplane was capable of carrying twelve passengers at 90 miles (144 kilometers) per hour. The Vimy, employed for use as a bomber by the British Air Force, could carry ten passengers after alterations.

Two acts by the United States federal government helped end the reliance on the war ghosts in the mid-1920s. The Kelly Act of 1925 transferred

Above: In the post World War I era, uses were even found for airplane's as simple in design as the Stearman biplane.

The airplane's range and utility grew with the introduction of multi-engine aircraft, such as the Ford Tri-Motor (opposite page) and the Fokker F-7 Southern Cross (right). Overleaf: The relative simplicity of the Fokker Southern Cross cockpit.

control of mail routes from the public to the private sector. The Air Commerce Act of 1926 allocated funds for the purpose of designing and building the infrastructure needed to ensure safe and efficient air service. The combination of these two acts helped increase the demand for new and improved aircraft that were specifically designed for civilian uses.

European manufacturers were the first to respond to the growing demand for nonmilitary aircraft. The Dutch built the Fokker F-2, a four-passenger, single-engine monoplane designed solely for nonmilitary use. In 1919 Germany debuted a classic commercial aircraft, the Junkers J-13. The J-13 held the distinction of being the first all-metal commercial airplane ever built. The single-engine monoplane contained six seats within an enclosed cabin. In 1925 the Ford Tri-Motor made its first appearance in America, and quickly gained a place in aviation history. In addition to being powered by three engines, the Tri-Motor carried fourteen passengers in a cabin completely encased in metal.

In the 1920s, the aviation industry in the United States began to emerge. With companies such as Boeing, Douglass, and Lockheed appearing on the scene, the rest of the world took notice. This was also a decade in which American aviators grabbed the international spotlight with daring aerial feats. None were more heroic than Charles Lindbergh's solo flight across the Atlantic in 1927. Aboard a Ryan monoplane loaded with sandwiches, but without the aid of a radio or sextant, Lindbergh left a Long Island airfield on May 20. Thirty-three hours and thirty minutes later, he touched down at Le Bourget, France, the first aviator to cross the Atlantic Ocean solo. Lindbergh became an immediate international hero. His accomplishment was a matter of great pride for America, which awarded him the Congressional Medal of Honor for his daring feat. It also served as a benchmark for other aviators to pursue and surpass. Indeed, just over one year later Charles Kingsford Smith and C.T.P. Ulm made the first flight between the United States and Australia aboard a Fokker F-7B, making only two stops in Honolulu and Fiji.

In the early 1930s, Amelia Earhart took a major step forward for the suffragette movement when she piloted a Lockheed Vega from Newfoundland to Northern Ireland in May 1932. Three months later she crossed the continental United States

from New York to Los Angeles without stopping. Both feats were firsts for women, and no doubt served to encourage young women and men to pursue the field of aviation.

Although scheduled airline service was slower in coming to the United States than it had been in Europe, the North American continent was not totally without its pioneer air carriers in the immediate postwar years. The first scheduled international air service in America was founded in November 1920, when Aeromarine West Indies Airways began service between Key West, Florida, and Havana, Cuba. Curtiss Flying Boats were used on this route, a practice that became widespread due to the lack of land-based airfields. A Curtiss NC-4 had proven the seaplane's reliability

© Charles E. Zirkle

in 1919 by crossing the Atlantic under the direction of A.C. Read. The Flying Boats of the 1920s fell out of favor in the late 1930s, since they were unable to reach landlocked cities, but not before the spirited production of some classic amphibious aircraft. In addition to the American-built Curtiss seaplanes, the twelve-engine Dornier Do X of Germany gained widespread use because of its capacity to carry over one hundred passengers. The Sikorsky S-42 became a popular long-distance carrier in the 1930s because of its ability to ferry thirty passengers up to 2,000 miles (3,200 kilometers).

One of the heaviest users of the Flying Boat era was Pan American Airlines. In fulfilling a strong desire by the United States government to link

© Terry Gwynn-Jones Collection

Smithsonian Institution

Two giants of American aviation. Amelia Earhart (above and right), the first woman to make a non-stop transcontinental flight, and Charles Lindbergh (far right), who made the first solo flight across the Atlantic in 1927.

FPG International

FPG International

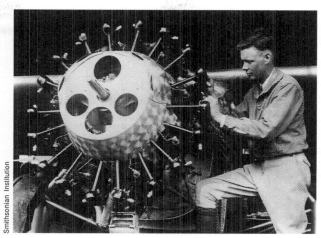

Amelia Earhart and her plane surrounded by admiring fans on a stop in California (top row, left). Top row, right: Lindbergh inspects the engine of his Ryan monoplane, the Spirit of St. Louis, (middle and below), now preserved as a historical remnant at the Smithsonian Institution's Air and Space Museum.

The jumbo aircraft of their day, the flying boats of Dornier (above) and Boeing (right) allowed newly created airlines such as Pan American (opposite page) to link people and places previously isolated from one another.

North and South America by air, Juan Trippe began building his global transportation empire in 1927. Tapping into his many contacts within the financial and governmental communities of the East Coast, Trippe was able to obtain the route authorization for service between mainland United States and Cuba. Having acquired control of Pan American World Airways, Trippe was further able to secure almost exclusive route authorizations for passenger and mail service between the United States and Latin America. Utilizing Fokker Tri-Motors and Sikorsky S-38 Flying Boats, Pan American quickly outgrew its inaugural Miami to Key West, Florida, service in 1927. By 1929, Pan American Airlines covered 15,000 miles (24,000 kilometers) in scheduled routes, well on its way to becoming the flagship American carrier around the world.

While Pan American's growth was impressive, by the mid-1930s the so-called trunk carriers of Europe were spanning the globe. KLM had linked Amsterdam and Jakarta by 1924, using Fokker single-engine aircraft. By 1934, the merger between Cie Franco-Roumaine de Navigation Aerienne and Cie Générale Aeropostale, resulting in the creation of Air France, had in succession linked Paris with Warsaw, Istanbul, Baghdad, and Saigon. The giant in the air, however, was England's Imperial Airways. Beginning in 1929, Imperial's Short Flying Boats eventually provided air service between London and India, Singapore, and Australia. Peaceful and productive uses for the airplane were now in full force around the world. It was to be a short-lived role, however, as war once again intervened, stealing the airplane away from its civilian uses.

LIFE

TRIPPE'S CLIPPER

PAN AMERICAN AIRWAYS SYSTEM

OCTOBER 20, 1941 **10** CENTS
YEARLY SUBSCRIPTION $4.50

REG. U. S. PAT. OFF.

TENTH YEAR OF PUBLICATION!

FICTION
MODEL
BUILDING
FACT

FLYING ACES

MARCH
15¢

報國 91

AUGUST SCHOMBURG

HOW JAPAN MIGHT ATTACK AMERICA

IF WAR STRIKES TOMORROW WILL AMERICA BE READY? ANSWERS BY AIR EXPERTS!
YOUR FICTION FAVORITES -- DICK KNIGHT, KERRY KEEN, PHINEAS
MODELS: SEVERSKY P-35, ATLANTIC CLIPPER, "DRAGON FLY" GAS JOB

c h a p t e r   s e v e n

THE AIRPLANE GOES TO WAR ... AGAIN

AMERICAN AIRLINES *Flagship* **FLIGHT REPORT**

DATE APRIL 20, 1945

ABOARD FLAGSHIP BOSTON

OUR POSITION: Over Moosup at 9:14 p.m. E.W.T.

ALTITUDE 2000 ft. above sea level 1985 ft. above the ground

TEMPERATURE at this altitude is 60 °F.

We are cruising at a SPEED of 135 mph

We are due to pass over HARTFORD approx. 10:11 p.m. E.W.T.

Ground temperature there is 53 °F.

REMARKS: WE HAVE JUST RECEIVED WORD THAT THE RUSSIANS HAVE ENTERED BERLIN.

CAPTAIN

FIRST OFFICER

STEWARDESS

PLEASE PASS THIS REPORT TO ANOTHER PASSENGER OR ASK THE STEWARDESS TO DO SO

AMERICAN AIRLINES, Inc.
ROUTE OF THE FLAGSHIP

AMAIR—
FORM T 70 B—6-44—700 BKS.—
PRINTED IN U.S.A.

While Flying Aces (opposite page) eerily foreshadowed events to come well before they occurred, airborne passengers on an American Airlines flight heard the welcome news of the war's imminent end while flying high above the ground (left).

Text vertical right side of image: FPG International

These Focke-Wulfe bi-planes (above) were rendered obsolete by the rapid advances made in aviation technology by the German Luftwaffe on the eve of World War II.

The invention of manned, powered flight was barely thirty-five years old on the eve of World War II. Yet, as the citizens of London and Dresden would soon find out, the airplane's capacity to deliver devastating blows from the sky was well advanced. While World War I had seen daring displays of aerial combat, civilians on the ground were relatively safe from the battles taking place in the sky. During World War I those on the ground had not been the principal targets of the combatant's aerial strikes. This was not true in World War II.

Advances in aviation technology were fast in coming during the six years of World War II. More armor, more firepower, and greater speed were the sole focus of aircraft designers from 1939 through 1945. Unlike World War I, in which aviation was dominated by personalities, the heroes of World War II were the airplanes themselves.

To a certain extent, the stage had been set for wholesale aerial warfare during the Spanish Civil War, which was fought from 1936 to 1939. The success and relative ease by which the German air force (called the Luftwaffe) was able to stage bombing runs on Spanish towns gave credence to Luftwaffe claims of air superiority. Indeed, German claims for air superiority were backed by speed records and precedent-setting developments. The Messerschmitt 109R set a new world record for speed in April 1939, by reaching just under 470 miles (750 kilometers) per hour. By the end of the year, the world's first jet-propelled aircraft, the Heinkel 178V1, had been unveiled by its German inventors. Clearly, the race for superiority in the skies was being won by the Germans quite handily.

Once the war began, the Luftwaffe did not have to wait very long to prove its claim as the best air force in the world. By September 1939, German bombing runs had dealt heavy blows to the Polish capital of Warsaw, battering the Polish government into complete submission. Despite suffering heavy losses in the air, German military planners deemed their blitzkrieg strategy a triumphant success. Based on a belief that quick and limited attacks by joint army and air force units are the most effective, blitzkrieg proponents won the first major battle of the war. As an air strategy, however, the blitzkrieg policy left the German air force almost totally lacking in its capacity to plan

and implement long-range bombing missions. Missing from the equation for such missions was the presence of a long-range bomber, a factor that would prove crucial in the closing years of the war.

Emphasis on dive-bombers, capable of making quick but short runs, led to the development of a series of aircraft known as Stukas. One of the early Stukas was the Junkers Ju-87 dive-bomber. Capable of reaching 200 miles (320 kilometers) per hour, the Ju-87 was a fixed-gear monoplane requiring a two-man crew. Appearing at the same

Descendants of earlier models tested in the air over England, the Messerschmitt Me-210 (left) and the Junkers Ju-88 (bottom) formed a potent pair.

A nemesis of the Luftwaffe was the Supermarine Spitfire (below) flown by members of the R.A.F. (Royal Air Force) squadron, whose insignia appears above.

time was the Messerschmitt 110, a twin-engine fighter-bomber with the capacity to reach 350 miles (560 kilometers) per hour. Having proven themselves capable of inflicting heavy damage, the Luftwaffe envisioned the Me-110 as a protective escort for their limited but devastating bombing missions. The attack on Rotterdam in May 1940 left few questions as to the airplane's destructive force. In a span of only five to ten minutes, forty Me-111 bombers killed 1,000 people, and left another 50,000 homeless.

While proving themselves effective at first, the Ju-87 and Me-110, eventually failed the Luftwaffe in the first major air battle of the war, the Battle of Britain. Commencing in early August 1940, the full-scale aerial assault on the British mainland by the Luftwaffe was devised as a prelude to an eventual land, sea, and air invasion of England. However, by mid-September it was clear that the plan had failed in its attempt to completely destroy the Royal Air Force (R.A.F.) of England.

While R.A.F. squadrons did indeed take heavy hits on the ground, two British fighters were able to inflict equal damage to the vaunted Luftwaffe. The Hawker Hurricane was a durable and highly maneuverable fighter plane capable of unleashing massive firepower from its twelve machine guns. The Supermarine Spitfire was also highly maneuverable, and capable of reaching speeds up to 350 miles (560 kilometers) per hour. A unique feature to the Spitfire was the ability to concentrate fire from its eight machine guns on a very small portion of a target. Because of its all-metal construction, the Spitfire proved a more difficult target to disable than its partially fabricated cousin, the Hurricane (built from metal and fabric).

By the end of August, the Hurricane and Spitfire had inflicted major damage on the German

Smithsonian Institution

© James N. Reuss

Capable of unleashing massive firepower, the Hawker Hurricane (left, both photos) was instrumental in the humiliation of the Germans during the Battle of Britain.

FPG International

While the Fiesler Storch (above) gave the Luftwaffe STOL (short take off and landing) capabilities, the Focke-Wulf 190 (right) provided them speed superiority in the skies over Europe.

fleet of Ju-87s, and the Luftwaffe had little alternative but to withdraw the *Stukageschwader* from the Battle of Britain. At the same time, the Me-110 was replaced by the Me-109 as the primary escort for German bombers. In just the month of August, the Luftwaffe lost over 270 bombers and 350 fighters. The Royal Air Force, too, suffered heavy losses—363 fighters in all—but the German goal of eliminating the R.A.F. altogether had failed. As a result, the Germans altered their strategy to focus on the night bombing of British cities. To

counter, the R.A.F. unleashed the Bristol Beaufighter in the closing days of the battle. The Beaufighter was a twin-engine, radar-equipped fighter that carried a crew of two. The radar enabled the Beaufighter to track Luftwaffe bombers at night. Nonetheless, the German bombing runs on British cities continued for several months, resulting in the heavy loss of life and property, but ending with no discernible blow to England's capacity for waging war. On the contrary, the English spirit carried them through the war.

Over the course of the war, both England and Germany developed innovative aircraft from their wartime assembly lines. In the never-ending effort to win control of the skies, German and British engineers put planes many years ahead of their time into battle. Some sparkled, but many fizzled; some of them literally.

German innovation was evident in the production of the Henschel 126 and the Fiesler Storch. The 126 was a high-wing monoplane utilized for photographic reconnaissance missions. The Storch turned out to be one of the earliest short takeoff and landing aircraft, or STOL. Deployment of STOL technology allowed the Luftwaffe to operate in areas otherwise limited to land or sea approaches. More conventional uses were intended for the Focke-Wulf 190 and the Messerschmitt 410 Hornet. At the time of its introduction in the summer of 1941, the Focke-Wulf 190 was the fastest fighter-bomber in the sky. Able to make quick and forceful strikes on England from bases in Germany, the 190 helped the Luftwaffe win back control of the skies over the English Channel. The Me-410 Hornet was a twin-engine fighter-bomber designed to destroy the heavily fortified bombers that appeared in Europe once the United States entered the war.

By war's end, German military strategists revealed two futuristic aircraft. The Messerschmitt 163 Komet was the only rocket-powered airplane to be used during World War II. Had the Komet been able to fulfill the desires of its creators, namely to speed through enemy fire and deliver explosives to a target, it might have altered the outcome of the air war over Europe. The Komet, capable of remaining aloft for ten minutes at best, exploded attempting to take off on many occasions, and in the final analysis was an insignificant contributor to the Luftwaffe. An aircraft that held greater promise for the Germans was the Messerschmitt 262 Swallow. The first operational jet-powered aircraft in the Luftwaffe inventory, the Swallow was designed as a high-speed fighter. Indeed, the Swallow's ability to reach speeds close

A first for the Luftwaffe, the Messerschmitt Me-262 Swallow (below) was powered by twin jet engines.

to 500 miles (800 kilometers) per hour made it a most formidable combatant. German military planners deployed it on most occasions as a bomber, however, and the Swallow never realized its full potential as a fighter.

For the most part, British aircraft designers were able to match the Germans plane for plane. The Hurricane and Spitfire had more than held their own against the German Me-109 and Me-110 during the Battle of Britain. The Beaufighter, while unable to effectively stop German bombing runs at night, did provide early-warning and interception capabilities for the Royal Air Force. In or-

Two British aircraft that carried the air war to the German cities were the Avro Lancaster (above and right), and the de Havilland Mosquito (below).

der for the British to launch their own long-range bombing missions, a series of bombers were developed by Avro. One of the most prolific bombers in this series was the Lancaster. Powered by four Rolls-Royce engines, the Lancaster was capable of delivering bombing payloads of just over 20,000 pounds (7,460 kilograms). First appearing in 1942, more than 7,000 Lancasters eventually rolled off of British and Canadian assembly lines.

Despite suffering major aircraft losses during 1941, the British military was able to remain competitive in the skies under difficult and seemingly impossible circumstances. A classic fighter-bomber emerged from one of the more dire circumstances, the lack of metal and other materials needed for aircraft manufacture. The de Havilland Mosquito appeared in the summer of 1941 as a versatile airplane capable of performing a wide range of missions. Owing to a lack of available metal, wood was used to construct the Mosquito. Nonetheless, with a top speed approaching 400 miles (640 kilometers) per hour, the Mosquito had three successful uses: as an unarmed bomber, a heavily armed fighter, and a high-performance re-

connaissance plane. The twin-engine plane realized an unexpected benefit from its all-wood frame, as the lack of a metallic fuselage made it more difficult for enemy radar to detect. The British even kept pace with the Germans in the area of jet-powered technology. In fact, the first operational British jet, the Gloster Meteor, saw limited action before the war came to an end.

While England and Germany engaged in air battles beginning in late 1939, the United States remained directly out of the air war until early December 1941. On December 7, 1941, Japan took steps that left the United States with no other option but to enter the air war, and eventually the war on land and at sea. The Japanese attack on Pearl Harbor not only caught the Allies by surprise, but with precious little information on Japanese aircraft and aviation technology. In the aftermath of Pearl Harbor, the United States learned that Japan possessed aircraft capable of inflicting devastating damage on Allied forces.

One of the Japanese carrier-based airplanes that carried out the assault on American naval forces in Hawaii was the Aichi Type 99. The all-metal dive-

The aircraft that brought the air war to American soil, the Japanese Zero (below). With removal of the "safety pins" (silhouetted below) from its payload of bombs, the Japanese Zero was armed for battle on American soil.

© Frank B. Mornillo

bomber was a single-engine, fixed-gear mono-plane armed with three cannons. Even more dev-astating blows were delivered by the Mitsubishi Type 0. The Zero was lightweight and much faster than the Aichi, with a maximum speed approach-ing 340 miles (540 kilometers) per hour. The Zero was also light on armor plating, leaving its fuel tanks susceptible to explosion. American pilots were unable to take advantage of the Zero's short-comings during the assault on Pearl Harbor, since they did not know this until after the assault. The

A Japanese collection of sky warriors: the Aichi Types Zero (below and opposite page, above), 6 (right), and the 99 Val (opposite page, below).

Japanese attack left massive destruction in its wake. All told, the Japanese lost less than thirty aircraft in the surprise attack on American soil, while destroying over 190 American planes, most of them while they were still on the ground. In ad-dition, eighteen ships were left dead in the water, and over 2,000 people were killed. Ironically, one of the main targets of the Japanese mission, American aircraft carriers, were not in port on that Sunday in December. This proved to be deci-sive in the eventual American victory in the skies over the Pacific.

The attack on Pearl Harbor began America's three-year entry into the war. It also set in motion an almost unbelievable display of industrial capac-ity by American men and women. In no other field was this industrial miracle more evident than in aviation. By all accounts, American success in the skies over the Pacific and Europe owe just as much to the miracle in the factories as they do to the pilots of the aircraft themselves.

At the outset of American entry into the war, the United States Army Air Corps was reliant upon two aircraft as fighters: the Bell P-39 and the

© Frank B. Mormillo

© William R. Wilson

While American air defenses began the war reliant upon the relatively primitive *Bell P-39 Airacobra* (above left) *and the Curtiss P-40* (above right), *the introduction of the Lockheed P-38 Lightning* (below) *and the Hamilton F4F* (right) *immediately gave United States aerial forces an aircraft equal to anything else in the sky.*

Curtiss-Wright P-40. The P-39 was a sluggish single-engine fighter, limited to flying at lower altitudes and lightly armed. The P-40 was also a lightly armed aircraft in its early form, but with added armaments in the post–Pearl Harbor period it became an effective exploiter of the Zero's weaknesses. American naval forces began the war with the Grumman F4F Wildcat as their main carrier-based fighter. While inferior to the Zero in raw performance capabilities, the Wildcat's durability and firepower led to numerous victories over the Japanese fighter in the Pacific.

During the winter of 1941, the United States Army Air Corps began taking delivery of the Lockheed P-38 Lightning. Evolving into one of the classics of the war era, the Lightning operated in all theaters as an interceptor, a fighter-bomber, and as a reconnaissance plane. The single-seater, built with twin engines and a twin tail assembly, operated comfortably at 20,000 feet (6,000 me-

ters), with a maximum speed of almost 400 miles (640 kilometers) per hour. Armed with four fifty-caliber machine guns and a twenty-millimeter cannon, the P-38 series saw extensive use as a fighter in the Pacific. Capable of being fitted with drop tanks, thereby increasing its range to 1,500 miles (2,400 kilometers), eventual Lightning models were also utilized in action as long-range fighter-bombers.

During the spring and summer of 1942, a succession of key air and sea battles took place in the Pacific. Emerging victorious from these battles was a group of American aircraft that played crucial roles in the effort to win back control of the Pacific theater. The Grumman TBM Avenger and the Douglas SBD Dauntless were the two main carrier-based attack planes during the battle for Midway. A so-called "wing-bender," the Avenger actually debuted as a torpedo and dive-bomber during the June 1942 battle for Midway. Despite

Crucial to the American victory in the Pacific were durable and versatile aircraft such as the Grumman TBM Avenger (below).

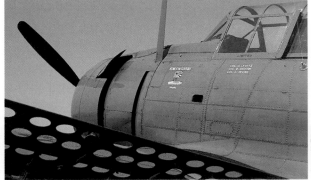

suffering initial losses to Japanese Zeroes at Midway, the Dauntless emerged as a potent weapon to aircraft in the air and to ships at sea. Configured to house a rear gunner as a member of its two-man crew, the Dauntless took credit for helping sink four Japanese carriers during the four-day battle at Midway. In addition, the Dauntless, the Avenger, and older aircraft such as the Grumman Wildcat and the Brewster Buffalo, helped United States aerial forces destroy almost 300 Japanese airplanes.

After regaining some control of the Pacific sea and air lanes, American forces were able to launch

Above: *United States Navy wings, a symbol of excellence and honor.* **Right and below:** *Feared in the air as well as at sea, the Douglas SBD-5 Dauntless left its mark throughout the Pacific.*

more ambitious aerial strikes against Japanese targets, including the island of Japan itself. By the end of 1943, American naval forces had all but secured the skies over the Pacific with the introduction of the Chance-Vought F4U Corsair and the Grumman F6F Hellcat. The Corsair had the distinction of being the heaviest carrier-based fighter built up to that point. Notwithstanding its immense size, the Corsair was fast, with a maximum speed of over 400 miles (640 kilometers) per hour, and was superior to the Zero in almost every respect. With six fifty-caliber machine guns and a launching capacity for eight five-inch (thirteen-centimeter) rockets, the bent-wing Corsair was a feared and deadly nemesis to Japanese air forces. Using a Zero captured in Alaska, Grumman engineers designed the Hellcat to exploit any and all weaknesses found in the Japanese fighter's design. The resulting carrier-based aircraft more than equaled its studied counterpart in the Pacific aerial battles of late 1943.

While the Corsair and Hellcat controlled the skies, American bombers were able to launch limited attacks on the Japanese mainland. The princi-

© James N. Reuss

© James N. Reuss

The SNJ-5 (above) was the plane used to train pilots during World War II. Unmatched in the air, the Grumman F6F Hellcat (middle), and the Chance-Vought F4U Corsair (below), provided superior air cover for United States Naval forces in the Pacific. Overleaf: Continuing what the Japanese began at Pearl Harbor on Dec. 7, 1941, the North American B-25 Mitchell carried the war to Japanese soil.

© Douglas A. Zalud

© Douglas A. Zalud

The machines which helped the Allied forces win the war included the Boeing B-25 (above), the B-17 Flying Fortress (right), and the Consolidated B-24 Liberator (opposite page, above). The spoils of victory are shown here: the Air Medal (opposite page, lower left), and the prized Distinguished Flying Cross (opposite page, lower right).

pal bomber in this strategy was the North American B-25 Mitchell. Devised as a smaller, so-called medium bomber, the twin-engine B-25 could carry only light payloads, but could pick up those payloads from the decks of American carriers based in the Pacific and deliver them where needed. Losses were heavy for the B-25 in bombing runs over Japan. The ability to strike deep into Japan's interior, however, provided Allied forces with a tremendous psychological victory.

While the aerial war in the Pacific targeted mainly naval vessels, the air war in Europe was land based, thereby requiring a different mission for the airplane. Rather than encounter Japanese fighters and naval vessels in limited engagements, aircraft in the European theater were required to make long-range bombing runs on land-based targets. Consequently, American military planners placed great emphasis on long-range bombers and high-performance fighter escorts.

Two of the more prolific American bombers built to fulfill this mission were the Boeing B-17

© James N. Reuss

Flying Fortress and the Consolidated B-24 Liberator. While pilots of both aircraft are still debating which was better, there is no doubt that both fulfilled their appointed missions with tremendous results. First appearing in Europe in 1942, the B-17 was a four-engine heavy bomber that saw extensive action on daylight bombing runs over Germany. Extremely durable even under heavy attack, the B-17 earned its nickname from the awesome amount of firepower it was capable of delivering in defense of itself. Outfitted with six pairs of fifty-caliber machine guns (in turrets located under, on top, and on both sides of the aircraft, in addition to the standard nose and tail turrets), the Flying Fortress was indeed just that. Its value as a bomber was greatly enhanced by its ability to defend itself from enemy attack without benefit of a fighter escort. Built in greater numbers in converted Ford automobile factories, the B-24 proved its worth as a heavy bomber in all corners of the world. While carrying a larger payload over greater distances than the B-17, the Liberator's only drawback was in its lower operating altitude. More susceptible to enemy ground fire and fighter attack, the B-24 achieved its greatest success on escorted bombing runs over German industrial cities.

Two fighters that provided escort service for Allied bombers were the Republic P-47 Thunderbolt and the North American P-51 Mustang. In many

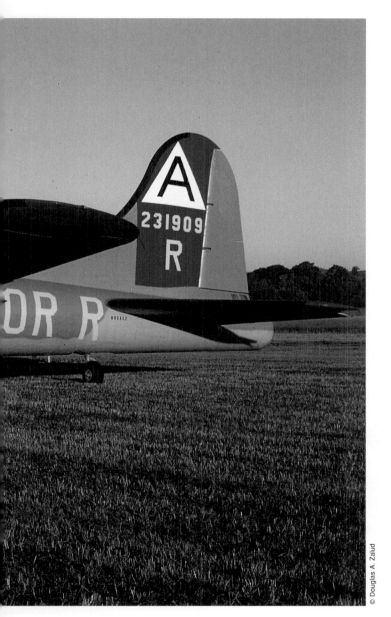
© Douglas A. Zalud

The Cadillac of the sky, the North American P-51 Mustang.

© James N. Reuss

© James N. Reuss

© James N. Reuss

© Douglas A. Zalud

© Phil Matt

ways the Thunderbolt and Mustang made heroes
out of Allied bomber pilots by providing extensive
and thorough coverage for United States and
R.A.F. bombing runs. Appearing first, the P-47
was a single-engine fighter made of a nearly im-
penetrable skin. With a top speed of over 400
miles (640 kilometers) per hour, and armed with
eight fifty-caliber machine guns, the P-47 realized
immediate success as a fighter and strafer, providing aerial support for ground troops. The Mustang
debuted shortly after the P-47, and realized the
same immediate success. Capable of operating at
ceilings exceeding 20,000 feet (6,000 meters),
the P-51 provided excellent escort capacity for
high-altitude, long-range bombers. With a maximum speed of almost 440 miles (700 kilometers)
per hour, the highly mobile P-51 also proved a
deadly foe for the Focke-Wulf 190 and the Mes-

**Combining the speed
and maneuverability
of aircraft, such as
the Republic P-47
Thunderbolt (above),
with the range and
bombing capabilities
of the Boeing B-29
Superfortress (right
and below right),
American aerial
forces proved them-
selves invincible on
two continents.**

FPG Interantional

serschmitt 109. All in all, the teaming of the heavy bombers with the agile, high-speed fighter escorts created a sure mix for certain Allied victory in Europe.

The final blow to the Axis powers was delivered by a heavy bomber of the United States Air Force, the Boeing B-29 Superfortress. Almost 100 feet (thirty meters) long, with a wingspan of 143 feet (forty-three meters), the B-29 was a long-range bomber capable of reaching Japan from captured territories in Saipan and Guam, over 1,000 miles (1,600 kilometers) away. The four-engine aircraft

featured the first pressurized cockpit, allowing crew members to remain conscious and alert even at high altitudes. With twelve fifty-caliber machine guns strategically located in turrets throughout the plane, the Superfortress was indeed a fortress in the sky. It was this plane that dropped the atomic bombs on the cities of Hiroshima and Nagasaki in August 1945, bringing the six-year war for world domination to a devastating end. For the first time in the history of the airplane the ability to control the sky meant the ability to control the world.

chapter eight

THE EARLY JET AGE

© Douglas A. Zalud

The end of World War II allowed for swift advances in jet-powered aircraft. Planes could now go farther distances faster than before.

With plenty of pilots and aircraft on hand following the end of the war, the commercial airliner quickly became a familiar sight in the skies over America.

I n many ways, World War II served to free aviation technology from the limitations placed upon it by the piston engine. The race to put the fastest fighter in the sky led aircraft designers on a frenzied pursuit of new and more effective sources of power. During the war, research on jet propulsion took giant steps in both England and Germany under the encouraging and anxious eyes of military planners. While jet-powered aircraft saw very limited action toward the end of the war, the advances in technology had laid the groundwork for the next phase in the evolution of the airplane, the jet powered commercial aircraft.

At the same time, the airplane's miraculous performance in World War II forever laid to rest skeptics of manned flight. That the airplane carried passengers farther, faster, and with greater efficiency than either the train or ocean liner was now an accepted fact. Flying had become an everyday occurrence for millions of combatants during the war, as they were shuttled around the globe aboard the mechanical birds of the sky. As these veterans returned home, it was only logical that they would expect the airplane to remain a part of their lives. In many ways, powered flight had gone from incredulity to commonplace.

To a certain extent, the commercialization of the airplane was a foregone conclusion once the war ended. Six years of unprecedented militarization on a global scale left the world with thousands of aircrafts and trained pilots. Planes such as the Douglas DC-3 had proven their stamina and

While surplus aircraft such as the Douglas DC-3 (above and opposite page, below) assumed important roles in the early days of commercial aviation, the advent of more advanced and specialized airliners such as the Lockheed Constellation (opposite page, above) brought the flying public into the airplane in droves.

durability in every conceivable wartime setting. With over 10,000 built during the war years alone, the DC-3 became a cheap way to enter the commercial aviation business, whether as a scheduled carrier, charter line, or freight hauler. With quickly expanding needs, however, American airline companies needed crafts that were faster and more capable of carrying more passengers over longer distances.

Aircraft built specifically for commercial use, such as the four-engine Lockheed 049 Constellation, were quick to appear once the war ended. Capable of carrying forty passengers at 350 miles (560 kilometers) per hour, the Constellation helped lead an explosion in air travel in the immediate postwar years. Despite its success, the market for medium- to long-range commercial aircraft

was dominated by the Douglas Company during the 1940s. Improvements to the DC-4, which first appeared in 1942, enabled the four-engine craft to haul sixty passengers at 250 miles (400 kilometers) per hour. By 1948, Douglas had put the DC-6 into service, a pressurized four-engine airplane that carried seventy passengers at almost 300 miles (480 kilometers) per hour. What the DC-4, DC-6, and Lockheed Constellation had proved was that the potential to make money flying passengers from one destination to another was indeed real.

The idea of attaching a jet engine to an airplane had been an old one. In fact, patents for various forms of jet propulsion had been granted as early as the Wright brothers' era. However, the basics for advancing this technology—heavy-duty com-

pressors and combustion chambers—along with the metal to construct turbine rotors, did not yet exist. Two early pioneers in the development of jet propulsion were A.A. Griffith and Frank Whittle, both of England. Griffith's idea for a primitive rotor blade was soon followed by his development of a gasoline turbine power source. By the latter years of World War II, Griffith had developed an operational turboprop, combining the propeller with the newfound power source. Going one step further, Frank Whittle concentrated his efforts on developing a turbojet. Beginning with an experimental model engine in 1937, Whittle's efforts eventually led to the development of the Gloster Meteor and to the pioneering jet engine work of Rolls-Royce.

Not to be forgotten was the even more advanced work on jet propulsion taking place in Ger-

many during the war. In late August 1939, the Heinkel 178V1 made the maiden voyage of a jet-powered aircraft. Three years later, the Messerschmitt 262 was flying under its twin-jet engine power. The German contribution to jet propulsion would be greater appreciated in the postwar years, as German scientists played key roles in the advancement of jet aircraft all around the world.

American advancement in jet engine technology is indebted to the voluntary contribution of German scientists after the war, as well as to the capture of German scientific documents. While Europe focused all financial resources on rebuilding its war-ravaged landscape, the United States was able to devote funding for further research and development on aircraft technology. As a consequence, America dominated the field of jet-powered aircraft technology well up until the early part of the 1960s.

Nowhere was this lead in technology more evident than in the application of jet power to military aircraft. The United States Air Force had entered the jet age in October 1942 with the successful flight of the Bell XP-59A. By war's end, the Lockheed P-80A Shooting Star had made its initial test flights, but did not become operational until several years later. In 1946, the P-80A made a decisive point in favor of jet technology by crossing the United States at an average speed of 550 miles (880 kilometers) per hour. Using captured research data on the German Messerschmitt 262, North American first flew the F-86 Sabre in October 1947. That same month, aboard the Bell XS-1, Major Charles E. Yeager became the first man to exceed the speed of sound in level flight. Less than a year later the Sabre itself attained supersonic speed, not in level flight, but in a dive.

FPG International

The days of propeller powered commercial aircraft such as the Douglas DC-6 (opposite page, above) were numbered with the advent of the jet engine. Borrowing on wartime technology first deployed in the Messerschmitt Me-262 (opposite page, below) and the Gloster Meteor (left), American aircraft designers asserted themselves in the post war period with the first airplane capable of achieving level supersonic flight, the Bell XS-1 (below).

FPG International

Above: Early American jet powered aircraft included the North American F-86 Sabre.

While jet technology centered on the fighter group, bombers were certainly not left out. In July 1948, the Boeing B-47 Stratojet, with its swept-wing design powered by six turbojets, appeared. The benefit of applying jet power to a bomber was immediately evident, as payloads of 20,000 pounds (7,460 kilograms) could now be carried in smaller and faster aircraft.

The newly applied jet technology received its first combat experience a mere five years after the end of World War II. The first jet-against-jet combat took place in the skies over Korea in November 1950, when a Soviet Mig-15 and an American Lockheed F-80 Shooting Star locked horns in combat. Once again, military struggle fed an un-

precedented surge in aircraft development, as the United States launched the Century series of fighters that controlled the skies for almost ten years. First in the series was the McDonnell F-101 Voodoo, for almost a decade the fastest plane in the world, topping out at 1,200 miles (1,900 kilometers) per hour. Eclipsing the Voodoo's speed in the latter part of the 1950s was the Convair F-106 Delta Dagger, the Lockheed F-104 Starfighter, and the Republic F-105 Thunderchief, all capable of achieving Mach 2 speed (twice the speed of sound).

The 1950s added three planes to the American arsenal of jet-powered aircraft. The Boeing B-52 Stratofortress served as the chief Strategic Air

FPG International

© James N. Reuss

Members of the United States Air Force Century Series of jet aircraft (from top to bottom): the McDonnell F-101 Voodoo, the Convair F-102 (inset), the North American F-100, and the Lockheed F-104 Starfighter. Jet power also came to naval air forces in the form of the F-2H Banshee (below).

© Andrew Ullrich/US Navy

Command bomber for the greater part of two decades after its debut in 1957. Powered by eight jet engines, the B-52's payload capacity exceeds 80,000 pounds (29,800 kilograms). Appearing a short while later, the McDonnell-Douglas F-4 Phantom series began its reign as king of the fighters in 1958. Tremendous climbing ability and speed well in excess of Mach 2 helped the F-4 hold a position of superiority as a fighter-bomber well into the 1960s. The third aircraft added to the American arsenal was the Lockheed U-2 reconnaissance craft, which became operational in 1957. Traveling at 500 miles (800 kilometers) per hour at 65,000 feet (20,000 meters), the U-2 led all other aircraft in its ability to fly undetected on intelligence-gathering missions.

While the lead in jet technology and its commercial applications was seized by the United States in the immediate postwar years, significant developments were taking place in Europe as well. The European domestic airline market was late in developing due to several factors: Unpredictable weather throughout Europe as well as the extremely short distances separating the major cities on the continent helped keep rail service alive and thriving as a means of transportation. Aircraft manufacturers realized that in order to compete with the train, a special aircraft would have to be tailor-made to fit the short-haul nature of European domestic travel. The Vickers Viscount 813 and the Fokker F-27 Friendship, both employing turboprop technology to carry passengers on smooth and quiet rides, were developed for the short haul.

Perhaps the greatest European achievement in the early postwar years came in the form of the

The devastating partnership of speed and payload in the jet age was epitomized by the Boeing B-52 Stratofortress (right, far right, and below).

© Douglas A. Zalud

© James N. Reuss

© James N. Reuss

© James N. Reuss

© James N. Reuss

The McDonnell-Douglas F-4 Phantom (above and left) was the king of the fighters, taking over where the B-52 left off.

Two familiar names from both wars and their peacetime offerings: the Vikers Viscount (above) and the Fokker F-27 Friendship (right).

world's first all-jet commercial airliner, the de Havilland Comet. Although Geoffrey de Havilland Jr., did not live to see the Comet in service, having been killed in 1946 in the crash of an experimental jet, the four-engine aircraft firmly placed the de Havilland name in aviation history. Entering service with the British Overseas Air Corporation in 1952, the Comet inaugurated the first scheduled jet airline service on its London-to-Johannesburg run. Carrying thirty-five passengers at nearly 500 miles (800 kilometers) per hour, the Comet's debut marked a milestone in commercial

jet travel. Problems with the aircraft were soon evident, as one fatal crash after another led to questioning of the plane's airworthiness. After successive disasters over the Mediterranean Sea in 1954, the Comet 1 series was grounded. Remains from one of the downed crafts revealed a crack in the fuselage that eventually ripped the airplane apart. Design changes were made, including strengthening the airplane's skin, and by 1958 the Comet 4 series of airliners were crossing the Atlantic. France debuted their own commercial jet airliner in 1955, the Aerospatiale Caravelle, gaining a share of the expanding global market.

By this time, the major players in designing and building jet-powered commercial airliners were emerging in America. The Boeing Corporation flew the prototype for its 707 model in July 1954. One year later, Pan American Airlines shocked the industry by announcing its goal of replacing its entire fleet of propeller-driven aircraft with jet-powered airplanes. At that time, Pan Am could choose from two very similar models, the Boeing 707 and the McDonnell-Douglas DC-8, both four-engine jet aircraft. In November 1958, Pan Am put the 707 into service for the first time. Powered by four Pratt and Whitney J57 jet engines, the 707 quickly put the excitement back into commercial flying. Never before could the average traveler experience such a work of aeronautical brilliance. Carrying up to 150 passengers more than 2,000 miles (3,200 kilometers), the 707 cruised at 575 miles (920 kilometers) per hour, at 30,000 feet (9,144 meters). A short time later, the DC-8 attained comparable levels of performance upon its entry into commercial service. American aircraft manufacturers had clearly seized the lead in the advancing technology of jet-powered commercial aircraft, a lead they would never relinquish.

With the early failures of the de Havilland Comet, and the continued fatal mishaps of the 1950s involving commercial aircraft of every sort, the airline industry was justified in viewing the jet with a great deal of caution and concern. The idea of taking responsibility for hurtling hundreds of people aloft at speeds approaching 600 miles (960 kilometers) per hour was at first glance insane. The thought that one could make money doing so seemed even more farfetched. But there were plenty of pioneers willing to take the risk. With the prospect of jet airliners multiplying traffic volumes while at the same time cutting costs, profit seekers got in line for the new-age jets rolling off the assembly lines in the late 1950s. To this day, that line is still forming.

Partners during wartime but rivals in peace, the earliest jet-powered commercial aircraft, the DC-8 from McDonnell-Douglas (below, top), and the 707 from Boeing (below, bottom), launched the two manufacturers on a long and intense competition for superiority in the global aviation market.

© Douglas A. Zalud

© Douglas A. Zalud

AN AIRPLANE IN EVERY DRIVEWAY

© James N. Reuss

Bent on duplicating the success of the Waco biplane (opposite page), and the Beech Staggerwing (left), general aviation companies saw the day in which the skies would be full of small aircraft.

© James N. Reuss

Above: An affordable alternative to land travel, the Piper Cub endeared itself to its owners much the same way the Ford Model T automobile had decades before.

The end of World War II brought great expectations for the continued expansion of general aviation, the field which encompassed all private, non-military uses of the airplane. With over ten million veterans returning home from the war, many of whom had become accustomed to traveling by plane, small aircraft manufacturers dreamed of putting an airplane in every driveway. With the educational and training benefits provided by the GI Bill, it was conceivable to assume that many of the veterans would use the funds to learn to fly. Many did, but not enough to allow aircraft manufacturers to compete with the automobile for the attention of the buying public.

It was not a lack of trying that prevented aircraft builders from placing an airplane in every driveway. The war was hardly over when manufacturers began advertising the virtues of owning your own airplane. In much the same way as the automobile had been promoted as a way of shrinking the world in the 1920s, in the 1940s the private airplane was touted as the way to bring the hardworking family closer to vacation spots near and far. Spending four hours aloft in a sleek, plush airplane was obviously preferable to traveling ten

hours in a hot, crowded car on summer vacation. Unfortunately for aircraft makers, a speedy, luxurious, and affordable airplane did not exist in the immediate postwar years, a fact consumers quickly realized.

The two-seat Piper Cub did sell for just shy of two thousand dollars in 1946, making it affordable for most middle-class consumers. The larger Stinson Voyager, which could seat four, sold for slightly more than five thousand dollars, an amount still within reach of the middle class. However, neither plane was very quick or luxurious. With both aircraft, the purchaser got durable, well-constructed airplanes, but little else. Just as they had done with the early automobiles at the turn of the century, in 1946 Macy's department store advertised the two-seater Ercoupe in their catalogue, for an affordable $2,900. For the wealthy consumer there was the Beechcraft Twin Beech, which sold for the costly sum of sixty thousand dollars.

The excitement of victory in Europe and the Pacific, coupled with the availability of affordable airplanes such as the Cub and Ercoupe, led to record levels of production in 1946—over thirty-three thousand small aircraft were sold. However, the number of small planes sold declined by 50 percent the following year, and by 1951 fewer than three thousand aircraft were being delivered annually to private owners.

There are many reasons for the steady decline in private airplane sales. The planes on the market that were affordable were also somewhat boring. To a buying public whose appetite for aerial excitement had been greatly increased during World War II, small aircraft that lumbered along at seventy-five miles (120 kilometers) per hour simply did not stir a great deal of interest. For those that climbed into the cockpit for test drives, the small private planes seemed more noisy and uncomfortable than the family cars on the market. At the same time, many of the more spacious and luxurious models were overpriced—a result of the unrealistic sales expectations on the part of the manufacturers. For the prospective buyer, choosing between a car and an airplane was facilitated by a lack of airports in which to land. The airplane manufacturers also received competition from an

Early multi-engine airplanes, such as the Beechcraft Twin Boanza (below), quickly gained acceptance in the military and civilian aviation market (left).

In a class by itself for many years, the Beechcraft Bonanza, built with an all-metal skin, brought luxury and high-performance to the private aircraft market.

unexpected source, the government. With over thirty thousand surplus aircraft available for sale in the postwar period, including many small models, buying an airplane new made little economic sense. All told, the private airplane makers found themselves in serious financial trouble by the end of the 1940s.

The manufacturers that survived the near collapse of the small plane market emerged stronger and more in tune to the needs of prospective buyers. Piper, Cessna, and Beechcraft survived by refocusing their design and manufacturing efforts. Designing and building aircraft tailor-made to fit the needs of the business pilot enabled them to meet the comfort and speed demands of the potential small-aircraft customer.

At Piper, the original Cub evolved into the speedier and more durable Super Cub. With a bigger engine, the Super Cub was able to operate from shorter landing strips, greatly increasing its versatility. In 1951, the company introduced the Tri-Pacer. With its plush interior and cruising speed of 130 miles (210 kilometers) per hour, the elder to the original Pacer became a favorite of early business pilots.

Cessna scored big with the 120/140 series of aircraft in the late 1940s. With its two-seat, side-by-side configuration, the 120/140 immediately became popular as a training aircraft. The 170 series of airplanes evolved into a popular business transport by the early 1950s. The four-seater was constructed totally from metal, thereby addressing the durability concerns of the business pilot. In addition, the 170A comfortably carried four passengers at 130 miles (210 kilometers) per hour, over a range of 700 miles (1,120 kilometers).

While Piper and Cessna survived by catering to the business pilot, it was Beechcraft that delivered the star of early private airplanes. In its early years, Beechcraft had limited success with the Staggerwing, a wood-and-fabric biplane. Then, in the late 1940s they introduced the Bonanza, which became a verifiable classic. Utilizing war-tested technology, the Beechcraft Bonanza put the private pilot behind the controls of an advanced, high-performance aircraft. With its distinguishing V-tail assembly, which greatly reduced weight and drag, the Bonanza immediately set itself apart from the rest of the small airplane family. The all-metal skin was further strengthened by the flush-riveting method employed in the plane's

While early twin engine aircraft like the Beechcraft 18 (below) were less than dazzling in appearance, airplane manufacturers soon offered the general aviation market models of sleek design and performance.

construction. Strong and stable, the Bonanza was also quiet, even while cruising along at a speed of 175 miles (280 kilometers) per hour. It was the first small plane to employ electric retractable landing gear in a tricycle configuration, further cushioning landings. With weather and navigational instrumentation standard, the Bonanza could transport four large business travelers over 700 miles (1,120 kilometers), day or night.

By the end of the 1950s, several classes of twin-engine planes had gained a foothold in the general aviation market. The most notable light twin was the Piper Apache, first appearing in 1953, which was capable of carrying five passengers at 170 miles (270 kilometers) per hour. Two years prior to the Apache, Aero introduced the Commander, a medium-size, twin-engine plane unique in its deployment of a high wing. Traveling at 200 miles (320 kilometers) per hour, the Commander's high-wing configuration provided its seven passengers with tremendous views and a great deal of comfort. The largest of the early twins was the Beechcraft Twin Beech, which ferried up to ten passengers at speeds exceeding 200 miles (320 kilometers) per hour. The growth of the twin-engine aircraft was a further response by the manufacturers to the needs and desires of the business community.

Left: Leading the way in design and performance was the Rockwell Commander, a medium-sized twin-engine plane that could travel up to 200 miles (320 km) per hour.

As with most advances in aviation, the stunts and feats of various pilots helped further the cause of the small, private airplane. In 1949, William Odom flew a Beechcraft Bonanza nonstop between Honolulu, Hawaii, and Teterboro, New Jersey, a distance of over 5,000 miles (8,000 kilometers). Five years later, it had become common practice for small twin-engine airplanes to be flown to their destinations across the Atlantic Ocean.

Several developments which promoted safer flying conditions outside the cockpit served to gain acceptance for the private airplane in the 1950s as well. The widespread placement of vertical omni-directional range (VOR) stations across the country allowed instrument-equipped planes to navigate on a nationwide scale. The development of ultrahigh frequency (UHF) radios further enhanced the private pilot's ability to communicate along static-free lines.

By the end of the 1950s, general aviation had begun to grow at the rate dreamed of by the manufacturers. Now, instead of an airplane in every driveway, there was a growing use of the private aircraft for a wide range of activities. The agribusiness community found many uses for the airplane, as did the forestry industry. Small aircrafts began linking remote communities in Alaska with one another, and delivered executives to business meetings in greater numbers. As an expression of individual interest and pleasure, the home-built and antique aircraft enthusiasts began reviving the classic airplanes of the two world wars. From the virtuous role of fire fighter to the illegal deployment as a contraband runner, the airplane had found a place in almost every sector of society.

c h a p t e r   t e n

A PEEK AT THE FUTURE

© Jon Reis

No longer merely a means of connecting faraway people and places with one another, the airplane now holds the promise of linking the planets to one another.

Designed with versatility of purposes in mind, the Boeing 727 (right) and 737 (below) series of aircraft will undoubtedly fly off into many more sunsets.

To a certain extent, we have already seen what airplanes of the future will look like. As with other forms of technologies, especially those related to transportation, the future depends a great deal on the needs of the present. The tremendous expense incurred in developing new aircraft acts as a barrier to research-and-development projects that hold little hope for practical use. Long gone are the days in which independently wealthy individuals toiled and tinkered to develop flying machines, like Louis Blériot had done in France at the turn of the twentieth century. Modern airplane development is a mammoth and costly undertaking, requiring the financial and technological resources found only in the halls of government and the giants of the aviation industry.

When Pan American World Airways began offering around-the-world flights aboard the Boeing 707 in 1959, many felt that aviation technology had gone as far as it could. Indeed, what else could possibly be gained from the airplane once the entire world had been linked by jet travel? However, the airplane held limitless potential in the minds of aircraft designers and engineers. Not content with having shrunk the size of the earth, aviation inventors set their sights on conquering the stratosphere, and beyond.

During the 1960s, developments in commercial air travel were fast and furious. Boeing followed its pioneering 707 with a succession of commercial aircraft, each addressing the needs of a changing environment for air travelers. In 1964, the 727 was put into service as a short- to medium-range transport, capable of carrying up to 150 passengers. By 1967, the prototype for the smaller, more fuel-efficient 737 was first flown. By the end of the decade, Boeing test pilots had flown the massive 747, the largest commercial aircraft in the world at the time. In a span of only ten years,

Boeing had presented the world with a wide range of airplanes, each crafted to meet a distinct niche in the exploding commercial aviation market.

While Boeing had established itself as the leader in the manufacture of commercial aircraft by the end of the 1960s, there were competitors to the throne. British Aerospace Corporation unveiled the BAC-111 in 1965. With the capacity for ninety passengers, and performance specifications similar to the 727, the twin-engine jet was a formidable alternative in the short-range market. That same year, McDonnell-Douglas debuted

their own short-range jet, the DC-9, a twin-engine jet that outperformed the BAC-111, and carried twenty to thirty more passengers. In 1967, the Dutch planemaker Fokker introduced their version of the short-haul jet, the F-28.

What the other aircraft manufacturers failed to do, however, was develop a full line of airplanes capable of meeting the specific needs of each and every airline. While McDonnell-Douglas, Lockheed, and the European consortium Airbus had all developed wide-body jumbo jets by the early 1970s (the DC-10, the L-1011, and the A-300 re-

Some of the legacies of European aviation: the British Aerospace 111 (below, top), the Fokker F28 Fellowship (below, middle), and the Airbus A-300 (below, bottom).

spectively), Boeing was far ahead in meeting the present needs of the airline industry as well as in planning for a changing future in the sky.

However, one area in which Boeing was not the leader was the development of a supersonic transport. As early as 1955, studies on developing commercial transports capable of exceeding the speed of sound were under way in England and in the United States. In 1960, France joined England in a joint effort to bring the SST (supersonic transport) concept to fruition, and indeed three years later the design for the Concorde was re-

vealed. Traveling near–Mach 2 speeds, the Concorde was conceived to carry just over one hundred passengers on trips of four to five thousand miles. In March 1969, the Concorde made its first test flight, and by the mid-1970s was linking London and Paris with points as far away as Rio de Janeiro, all in a matter of a few short hours. At the same time, Boeing terminated its own SST program, seeing it as too costly, with little hope of ever becoming profitable.

While aircraft such as the Concorde and the 747 certainly offer glimpses of the commercial future

Below: *The crown jewel of Europe's quest for the sky, the Concorde.*

Right and below: *The Lockheed C-5 Galaxy. The body of the plane was longer than many of the Wright brothers' first flights!*

for airplanes, the military aircraft of the 1970s and 1980s reveal the more exciting and adventurous possibilities for the Wright brothers' invention. As the largest airplane in the world at the time of its introduction in 1970, the Lockheed C-5A Galaxy fills a very practical need for the United States Air Force, with its capacity for hauling a massive array of troops and armaments over a 3,000-mile (4,800-kilometer) range. The SR-71 reconnaissance plane looks and performs like a vision from the future, with its exact performance specifications known only to the military. Appearing in public for the first time in 1989, the B-2 Stealth bomber bears a striking resemblance to the World War II–era Flying Wing. The genius of the B-2 is hidden, literally, in the sense that the airplane's construction leaves it undetectable by enemy radar. The

application of stealth technology to other aircraft will change the face of aerial warfare in the future.

Outside of the never-ending military quest to design and build a superior air force, the peaceful future for the airplane is tied to the needs and demands of the traveling public and to the restrictions placed on those needs by the public. Several factors in air travel are indisputable, beginning with the fact that as a means of transportation, the airplane is far superior to any other mode in delivering passengers to their destination quickly and safely. As a consequence, air travel is sure to continue growing, as witnessed by the record number of aircrafts being ordered by the major airlines in the late 1980s. At the same time, concerns over the negative environmental impact of air travel are also growing. Groups demanding quieter, cleaner,

Below: *As futuristic looking as it is, the Lockheed SR-71 reconnaissance plane is a victim of obsolescence, replaced by advanced satellite technology. Overleaf: The next generation of aircraft is here: The space shuttle Columbia waits on its launch pad for its next mission.*

Courtesy Lockheed

© James N. Reuss

and more fuel-efficient aircrafts have grown in number and political power.

For the most part, aircraft manufacturers have been able to meet these demands. With the introduction of the MD-80 series, McDonnell-Douglas has surpassed federally mandated noise-reduction requirements at selected airports in the United States and abroad. With many airports sharing space with bordering residential developments, the need for quieter aircraft is crucial to their continued growth and expansion. The implementation of the "hub and spoke" system by most of the major airlines (in which service between cities is routed through hub airports, rather than being connected by direct link), puts the emphasis on carrying the greatest number of passengers on each and every flight. The need to increase seat

With an eye toward the future, Boeing has launched the next generation of aircraft in their fleet, the 757 (above). At the same time, it has improved and changed the 747 (right), allowing it to carry more passengers greater distances.

capacity, while at the same time reducing fuel consumption, has resulted in the development of Boeing's 757 and 767 series of aircraft. Both operating on two engines, the 757 offers seating for up to 230 passengers, while the 767 can seat 290. Aircraft such as these give airlines maximum load capacity while greatly reducing fuel consumption. It is almost certain that the next generation of passenger aircraft will follow the same pattern.

With more airplanes in the sky than ever before, the airways have become congested with aircraft of all sorts. Many transportation planners have called for the construction of mega regional airports, far removed from urban areas, with the sole purpose of acting as a way station for air travelers. In such a scenario, jumbo aircraft from the West Coast would deliver passengers to a mega airport in an Iowa cornfield, for example, at which point they would transfer to other jumbo aircraft for delivery to various points in the East. If these ideas are adopted, we will surely see crafts even larger than current 747 models capable of carrying four hundred passengers.

For inner-city airports, the noise and congestion problem is most severe. Increasing air traffic, coupled with rising demands for less noise and pollution, will result in greater implementation of restricted take off and landing rules. Designing aircraft capable of operating on shorter runways, with greater climbing ability, will be important in meeting RTOL guidelines. The British Aerospace 146 series provides an early look at a jet aircraft capable of operating out of cramped and crowded airfields.

While the long-range feasibility of commercial supersonic transportation is still being debated, the United States and the Soviet Union have gone one step further in the development of Space Shuttle technology. With the ability to take off on earth, circle the globe outside of earth's atmosphere, and return to land in a reusable aircraft, scientists at NASA have given the rest of the world reason to hope that someday interplanetary travel will become a reality. For Leonardo da Vinci, who simply wanted to soar with the birds, and Orville and Wilbur Wright, whose determination proved man smarter than the birds, taking the airplane into space is a fitting and conquering tribute with endless possibilities in store.

Below: *The Cessna Citation is the ultimate in private plane luxury.*

BIBLIOGRAPHY

Andrews, Allen. *The Flying Machine: Its Evolution Through the Ages.* New York: G.P. Putnam's Sons, 1977.

Angelucci, Enzo. *World Encyclopedia of Civil Aircraft: From Leonardo Da Vinci to the Present.* New York: Crown Publishers, Inc., 1982.

Bilstein, Roger E. *Flight in America 1900–1983: From the Wrights to the Astronauts.* Baltimore: Johns Hopkins University Press, 1984.

Bilstein, Roger E. *Flight Patterns: Trends of Aeronautical Development in the United States, 1918–1929.* Athens, Georgia: University of Georgia Press, 1983.

Corn, Joseph J. *The Winged Gospel: America's Romance With Aviation, 1900–1950.* New York: Oxford University Press, 1983.

Crouch, Tom D. *A Dream of Wings: Americans and the Airplane 1875–1905.* New York: W.W. Norton and Company, 1981.

Degen, Paula, and Lynanne Wescott. *Wind and Sand: The Story of the Wright Brothers at Kitty Hawk.* New York: Harry N. Abrams, Inc., 1983.

Francis, Devon. *Power to Fly: A History of the Oil and Aviation Partnership.* Hong Kong: Aero Publishers, 1985.

Gunston, Bill. *Aviation: The Complete Story of Man's Conquest of the Air.* London: Octopus Books, Ltd., 1978.

Gunston, Bill and Frank Howard. *The Conquest of the Air.* New York: Random House, 1972.

Hart, Clive. *The Prehistory of Flight.* Berkeley, California: University of California Press, 1985.

Jablonski, Edward. *Man With Wings: A Pictorial History of Aviation.* Garden City, New York: Doubleday and Co., 1980.

Mason, Francis K. and Martin C. Windrow. *Air Facts and Feats: A Record of Aerospace Achievement.* Garden City, New York: Doubleday and Co., 1970.

Mason, Francis K. and Martin C. Windrow. *Know Aviation: Seventy Years of Man's Endeavor.* Garden City, New York: Doubleday and Co., 1973.

Moolman, Valerie. *The Road to Kitty Hawk.* Alexandria, Virginia: Time-Life Books, 1980.

Prendergast, Curtis. *The First Aviators.* Alexandria, Virginia: Time-Life Books, 1980.

Shephard, Peter, and John Young. *Aircraft: The Story of Powered Flight.* London: Ward Lock Limited, 1972.

Wragg, David W. *Flight Before Flying.* New York: Frederick Fell Publishers, Inc., 1974.

INDEX